LETTERS

FROM ROME AND BEYOND

Gerald O'Collins, SJ, AC

Connor Court Publishing

CONNOR COURT PUBLISHING PTY LTD
PO Box 7257
Redland Bay QLD 4165
sales@connorcourt.com
www.connorcourtpublishing.com.au

Cover image: Meeting Pope John Paul II. Photo taken from *On the Left Bank of the Tiber.*

ISBN: 9781922449528 (pbk.)

Cover design by Maria Giordano

Printed in Australia

I dedicate this book to

Martin and Tessa de Bertodano

and their wonderful extended family.

The collected letters of eminent theologian, Fr Gerald O'Collins SJ, present a wonderfully vivid insight into his life, his teaching and his writing. From Rome to the USA, from England to Australia, his native land, we read of the many extraordinary people he met, the warmth of his wider family life, the depth of his theological insights, his sense of humour and, above all, his remarkable capacity for friendship at every level. This is a gripping collection that makes for enjoyable and inspiring reading.

- Prof Dorothy A. Lee, FAHA, Trinity College, University of Divinity

PREFACE

My Mother and my three older sisters (Moira, Dympna, and Maev) were inveterate writers of letters and postcards. They also kept what I mailed to them over many years and from different parts of the world.

After Moira died in October 2017, the boxes in which she had stored my correspondence were passed on to me. They held over a hundred letters and a few postcards written during more than thirty years of living at the Pontifical Gregorian University in the heart of old Rome (1974–2006).

I had just completed transcribing this family correspondence when a trove of letters (from 1995 to 2013) arrived from Jane Steingraeber, a friend who lives in La Crosse, Wisconsin. I am most grateful to Jane for making these further letters available.

How did I experience more than three decades of teaching and writing theology in a very international university (founded in 1551) at the centre of Catholic Christianity? *On the Left Bank of the Tiber*[1] gave a fully deployed answer to that question. But there is room also for the correspondence generated by the Roman experience and its aftermath. Letters capture things more vividly and directly. They turn the searchlight on events in real time, rather than in retrospect. These letters blend public news of state and church with personal

---

1   Brisbane/Leominster: Connor Court/Gracewing, 2013.

details of interaction with family, friends, and others.

The letters provide an unflinching account of teaching not only in English but also in Italian, of working to renew the faculty at the Gregorian, and of supervising research students from all over the world. Eventually I directed hundreds who wrote a master's dissertation and ninety-two who successfully completed their doctorate under my supervision. The correspondence also reflects progress in writing not only works of professional theology but also spiritual books of a popular nature.

"All roads lead to Rome," as the classical proverb tells us. An extravagant parade of visitors filled my years in the eternal city. The letters document meeting those who began arriving from the mid-seventies.

Within Rome itself new relations opened up: with those who staffed colleges and embassies; with Italian families; with the Vatican Radio, the BBC, and other networks. The letters also describe what I did during summer vacations—on lecturing and teaching tours which could take me to every continent.

Some letters to Jane, written after I left Rome for London (2006–2009) and Melbourne (from late 2009), picture the aftermath of more than three decades on the left bank of the Tiber. Christmas letters and other letters fill out the post-Rome story down to 2020.

Re-reading all these letters, sometimes more than forty years after I wrote them, brought back in a fresh way a host of people, events, and insights. I hope readers may share something of those experiences. I dedicate this book to Martin and Tessa de Bertodano and their wonderful extended family. My warm thanks go out to Anne Hunt, Brenda Niall, Isaac Demase, and others whose advice, example and help encouraged me to put this book together.

The original letters are now all kept in the archives of the Australian Jesuit Province (Hawthorn, Victoria).

Gerald O'Collins, SJ, AC

Jesuit Theological College,

Parkville, Australia.

17 March 2021.

CONTENTS

Part I:
The Final Years of Pope Paul VI
(1974–1978)

Via Silvio Spaventa [a Jesuit residence], Florence, August 11, 1974.

[This letter to my sister Moira refers to two of her eight children, Bronwen and Mark, and to our aunt, Mary Lewis.]

Dear Moira, Thank you for your letter which was waiting for me when I returned from my two weeks at a Faith and Order meeting at the University of Ghana in West Africa (July 22–August 5). I wrote reports for various papers (including *The Australian*, *The Advocate*, and *The Tablet*). So you can read my impressions, provided one of these papers prints them.[2] The only Ghanaian I know happened to be away from the university—on sabbatical leave.[3] But no matter, as the participants included Jürgen Moltmann from Germany, Eduard Schweizer from Switzerland, and some other friends.

Please congratulate Bronwen on her skiing success and

---

2   My articles appeared in *The Tablet* (August 24, 1974), *Doctrine and Life* 25 (1975), *Theological Studies* 36 (1975), and *Unitas* 30 (1975).

3   John Pobee, who studied at the University of Cambridge in the 1960s.

wish her a happy birthday on August 20, as well as Mark on September 1. If you have Mary Lewis's new address, could you send it to me please. I take it that she has moved by this time from Wyagdon Street. Is the new Archbishop of Melbourne Frank Little? [He was.] I have been out of circulation either in Ghana or in Florence since the last days of June. Although both places are extremely pleasant, Australian news is not plentiful.

For the thirtieth anniversary of the liberation of Florence, Field Marshal John Harding (who in the summer of 1944 commanded the British forces in the area) came this weekend. He was standing with some Italian generals and alongside the British consul (Hebblethwaite, a Pembroke College, Cambridge University man) at the Mass which Cardinal Florit celebrated in the Piazza della Signoria this morning. I found myself with a group of Communists who shoved clenched fists in the air during some introductory music, held up a huge notice proclaiming peace and progress through their party, and generally seemed like a group of Young Catholic Workers. Hundreds of police of all kinds everywhere. The neo-Fascist bombings, up to the latest massacre on a train, have created some tension and a great deal of anxiety to see all the terrorists arrested.

After the Mass I walked off to visit the grave of Elizabeth Browning in the English cemetery, now the property of the Swiss government. I pulled the bell-cord; an old lady came to let me in. I found the Browning grave very easily, the only one with fresh flowers growing alongside and with other flowers in a vase.

This weekend brass bands from all over Tuscany have

descended on Florence. Last night I heard a concert from one of them—in front of the Church of San Lorenzo. The excellent program included pieces from *The Merry Widow* and *The Dance of the Hours*, but the overwhelmingly Italian audience offered only mediocre applause at the end and only relative silence during the performance. I guess that a conductor knows that he has really led a superlative performance when Italians give him total silence and thunderous applause. Australians must be too easily pleased.

Moira, would you do me a favour and get refunded by Mother when she returns? She offered to buy me a typewriter at the end of summer, but in fact I will be given one anyway. What is needed, though, is payment for my expenses in Ghana: $168 (US). What is that in Australian dollars? $110? I would be grateful if you could send this to Mrs Renate Sbeghen, World Council of Churches, Commission on Faith and Order, 150 Route de Ferney, Geneva, Switzerland, saying that this covers my bill for the Ghana meeting. You can recoup the same from Mother when she returns. Thanks for this.

On August 31, I leave for Rome to take up residence at the Gregorian. Classes start early in October. Next (European) summer I will teach at a summer school in Vermont (June 15–20), and hope to reach Australia in July or August—perhaps via the World Council of Churches General Assembly in Jakarta—before returning to Rome in September.

My love to all, Gerald.

[I neglected to mention that, while I was still in Florence and had not yet left for Rome, I had afternoon tea with Giorgio La Pira (1904–1977) at the Dominican Convent of San Marco, where he lived. Sicilian by birth, he had served for years as Mayor of Florence

(1951–57 and 1960–64). He dedicated his life to helping the poor, to peacemaking between nations, and to dialogue with those of other religious beliefs. Every inch an Italian, he told me: "Father Gerald, you realize that Europe is the centre of the world, Italy is the centre of Europe, and Florence is the centre of Italy." Before I left San Marco, he showed me paintings by Beato Angelico and the cell occupied by the religious reformer, Girolamo Savonarola (1452–1498). He insisted on taking my arm and walking me home to the Jesuit residence in the Via Silvio Spaventa. His final advice was: "When you go to Rome, don't rock the barque of Peter." On July 5, 2018, the Vatican recognized his heroic virtues—a necessary step on the way to possibly being beatified and canonized.]

Gregorian University, Rome, September 15, 1974.

[This letter refers to my nephews, Nicholas and Les Coleman, Sue, the wife of Les, my niece Marion Peters, Kevin Coleman, husband of my sister Dympna, and the Australian journalist Desmond O'Grady.]

My dear Mother, Thank you for your letter from Heathrow. I hope the home run via Zambia went off very happily.[4] I will drop a note to Nicholas in London.[5]

The students don't arrive back before early October, and my own classes won't begin until October 18. But I am glad to have the time to put my lectures into Italian. The weather continues to be magnificent—warm days and cooler evenings. The president's palace is right behind the Gregorian; every

4 After visiting Europe, Mother had been staying in Zambia with her grandson, Les Coleman, and his wife Sue.
5 Having picked up a tropical disease en route to London, Nick found himself confined to the Hospital for Tropical Diseases St Pancras. A few years later, he would study (successfully) for a PhD in theology at the University of Cambridge.

afternoon the band plays for the changing of the guard. There are still a few knots of tourists in town. At the Gregorian itself the professors continue to return, after a summer spent back in their own countries, teaching in the United States, etc. My Italian has come along well enough to enable me to preach and hold reasonable conversations in that language.

The conference in Ghana proved even better than I expected. A large number of old friends like Moltmann attended, and I was delighted to be able to get to know a good range of people from the third world. *The Tablet* for August 24 carried a report I wrote on the meeting. I also sent pieces to *The Advocate*, *The Australian*, and some other Australian papers, but have no idea whether or not they used them.

The World Council of Churches planned to hold their Fifth General Assembly in Jakarta next year, but that has had to be changed. Now the WCC are to meet in Nairobi in November or December 1975. With luck I may make that meeting and be able to visit Zambia, if Les and Sue are still there. [Les was working as an engineer for copper mines in Zambia.]

So far I haven't ventured out to see Desmond O'Grady, Cardinal James Knox etc., but must get round to that soon. I have been busy finding out how the libraries run, getting hold of a dentist to replace a filling which decided to drop out, and generally do all the other things which one does to settle into a new environment. My love to all at home. Please wish Marion and Kevin a happy birthday from me on October 2. Love, Gerald.

Gregorian University, Rome, November 20, 1974.

[This letter refers to my sister Maev, Mother's new home, Glynneath (on the same property as her earlier home, Rock Lodge), to SVDs, members of the Society of the Divine Word, and to Stephanie, the wife of my brother Glynn.]

Dear Mother, Maev, Moira et al., Happy Christmas to you all. Please pass this letter on to Moira, provided, of course, it first arrives safely at Glynneath. Talking of Glynneath, I would like to have had a copy of Cicero from the library shelves last Sunday. Sunshine was pouring down when I climbed my way up to Tuscolo (above Frascati) to visit Cicero's villa and the exquisite little theatre that rests almost at the top of the hill.

Yesterday I delivered my 14th lecture in Italian. That means that there are only thirteen more to go before Christmas, and after that I teach in English for the rest of the year. The class seems to put up with me happily. Mainly seminarians (some of whom are only twenty), the class includes a doctor retired from the Italian army, several nuns, and some ladies in lay dress (whom I suspect of also being nuns). One hundred and fifty, all told. I have been visiting the national colleges to meet them in smaller groups: the English College, the German College, the Augustinians (Irish and Australian), the North American College, and tomorrow the Seminario Romano (where Pope John XXIII studied).

A pleasant Italian dropped in the other day to tell me that his firm (Cittadella) will put out next April a translation of *The Easter Jesus*, and are interested in doing a translation of *Has Dogma a Future?* (The latter opus comes out next January.) I asked Darton, Longman & Todd to send a copy to Glynneath. It should arrive by the end of February. Speaking of books, the wretched Mercier Press in Cork still refuses to answer my letters or let me see *The Theology of Secularity*, a paperback which, I gather, is already on sale in Melbourne. It marks a change in my whole approach to theology and perhaps to life itself—by including jokes. Theology is too serious. But you don't have to laugh or even smile at the jokes, if you don't care for them. Father John Arnold Phillips wrote the other day to let me know that Polding Press (the press connected with the Central Catholic Library) should publish before Christmas grandfather's letters and *Faith Under Fire*. The letters probably need some pushing, publicity etc. Fr Phillips told me that he would phone Steph to see whether she would still be able to offer the book a small launching party. But let the faith book take care of itself.

After this burst of publishing, I have no intention of curbing my attempt to further the world's paper shortage. But it may be late 1975 before my next book (on Christ's death), *The Calvary Christ*, gets finished, and it could not be published before late 1976.

News here is mostly public: the new Moro government, Henry Kissinger's visit, a wave of kidnappings etc. I see a bit of Desmond O'Grady, and took his nine-year-old daughter, Donatella O'Grady (marvellous name!), to the zoo a couple of weeks back. Cardinal Knox I will see during the Australian get-together at Propaganda on December 1. When I reached Rome, I dropped him a line, but with the bishops' synod and other matters he was rather busy. By the way, Maev, your friend, Annette Auguste, from the UN (on her way from Papua New Guinea to somewhere in Africa) phoned—cheerfully—when she passed through Rome. Recently at Nemi, when I lectured to them on Christ, I saw some of the SVDs from Mt

Hagen, Wewak, and other places in Papua New Guinea. Love to all, Gerald.

[After doctoral studies at Columbia University, New York, where she made friends with Annette Auguste from the West Indies and many others, my sister Maev joined the newly opened University of Papua New Guinea in 1972 to establish a social work program.]

Gregorian University, Rome, January 1, 1975.

[This letter refers to the home in Orrong Road, Melbourne, where my sister Moira, her husband Jim and their eight children lived, and to Patrick O'Sullivan, the provincial superior of the Australian Jesuits.]

My dear Mother, A very happy New Year to you! Good wishes are still valid until the first is over. In the excitement of the phone call today to Orrong Road, I forgot to mention that I will definitely be out in Australia—next August and for the beginning of September. The program runs like this: leave Rome early June to teach for a week at an institute in Burlington (Vermont), arrive in New Zealand via the West coast of the United States about June 26, teach in Dunedin for the Catholic and Presbyterian theological colleges and the University of Otago till about August 9, then come across to Melbourne for some weeks before returning in easy stages (Canberra, Sydney, Brisbane, and Manila) to Rome about September 25.

The Holy Year got away to a good start on Christmas Eve. The ceremonies, the huge crowd, the Pope sticking at it all despite his arthritis, and the rest made it a moving occasion. It also looked like a throw-back to the days of the papal monarchy with Roman nobles, men with chiselled faces and medals thumping on their chests, directing the crowd inside the basilica.

Last Sunday I went up to Orvieto for the day, and saw the church where Boniface VIII canonized King Louis IX of France. Boniface was a strange mixture. Among other things, he was the pope who started the holy year practice in 1300, and also the pope who issued *Unam Sanctam*, the most titanic claim to papal authority the world has ever seen. Orvieto is crammed with memorials of the past: the pulpit from which Thomas Aquinas taught, the crucifix which is supposed to have said to him, "Thomas, you have spoken well of me," St Patrick's Well built by Clement VIII (d. 1605), Etruscan tombs etc.

After classes ended on December 21, I saw a few of the plays the students put on for the Christmas season: the pantomime ("The Three Musketeers") at the English College, "The Pirates of Penzance" at the Scots College, and "Pool's Paradise" (a farce) at the Augustinian College. Christmas offers a good chance of meeting various members of the English-speaking community in Rome. The British ambassador to the Italian Republic, who happens to be a member of Pembroke College (Cambridge), was at the English College pantomime. So I was able to give him the latest news from there.

I have been seeing a good deal of Fr Pat O'Sullivan during our Jesuit general congregation [which corresponds to the general chapter in some other religious institutes]. Next Monday we will have dinner together, with an English Jesuit friend [Myles Lovell] who is off to run a seminary in southern Sudan.

I hope my edition of grandfather's letters has hit the streets now, and that you like the production. Probably I won't see a copy myself before March. Once the Suez canal gets opened, that will speed up surface mail. I fear that the next Arab-Israeli war, however, might just coincide with the re-opening. But let's not be pessimistic. Much love, Gerald.

Gregorian University, Rome, January 23, 1975.

[This letter refers to the unexpected death of Kevin Coleman, a County Court judge who was my sister Dympna's husband, and to the birthday of my eldest nephew, Stewart Peters, soon to visit Rome.]

My dear Mother,

Your letter of December 30 (which mentioned how sick Kevin was) reached me only on January 18. So it was quite a shock when Dympna's telegram arrived on January 8, telling me of his death. I'll miss his kindly, cheerful presence when I get back later this year. God love him. RIP.

On Tuesday night I was out at the Beda College giving a lecture on Christ's death. The oldest student there is an American aged seventy. So the tradition of late vocations is being preserved happily. I ran into a New Zealander from Dunedin. Now that I am going to Dunedin for six weeks or so, people from there are popping up constantly. On Sunday last an Australian friend (who teaches at La Trobe University in Melbourne) asked me to dine at the British School, and there was a lecturer in classical archaeology from Dunedin!

Last night I inaugurated a seminar for the students who are writing their doctorates with me: four Americans [Daniel Kendall, Vincent Malatesta, Frank Virgulak, and Andy

Hohman], one Englishman, an Indian [Ravi Santosh Kamath], a Croat [Nikola Dogan], and an Italian [Claudio Delpero]. We went on to dine together at a cheap *trattoria*, la Maddalena, afterwards. The mood was exuberant, and I hope the result will be quite a bit of mutual help, even if some of them are writing on every different subjects.

A hard week of exams opens for me on February 3; then there's a free week; and classes start again on February 17.

Doubtless this won't reach you before Stewart's birthday. But do wish him the best from me retrospectively. Preparations are already being made to welcome him to Rome. Much love, Gerald.

Gregorian University, Rome, February 23, 1975.

[This letter refers to an Irish cousin, Eleanor Harbison, and her husband Jock.]

My dear Mother, Bishop Philip Kennedy from Adelaide, for four years a fellow boarder with me at Xavier College [Melbourne], is here in Rome for a month. With others I have been helping to entertain him between his working engagements. This weekend he has gone down to Calabria to visit the families of Italian migrants he knows in Adelaide. On Tuesday I will take him to lunch at the Bellarmino, a college for over one hundred young Jesuit priests in graduate studies. On Wednesday we join Patrick O'Sullivan for Mass in the rooms of St Ignatius Loyola, to be followed by lunch at the International College of the Gesù. Philip is just as nice as he ever was. I rather like introducing him to Americans and others—to show what an Australian bishop can be like.

The second semester got under way last Monday. Over seventy students are taking my course on Christ's death and resurrection. The semester runs through until the end of May, with a couple of weeks off at Easter.

Plenty of gossip about the Holy Office's admonition to Hans Küng which came out last week. Cardinal König of Vienna, speaking in German over Vatican Radio, reported how in his experience Küng's latest book, *On Being a Christian*, has brought a thousand people back to the practice of the Christian faith. A member of the Holy Office I know well [Eduard Dhanis, SJ] was furious at the Cardinal's saying this: "a lot of stupid nonsense." But good old König!

After this letter I must write one to an Anglican priest who is just about to become a Catholic. [Eventually, he decided not to take the step.] In England this still means giving up his priestly work and turning to teaching or some other related profession. But I must point out to him that two or three Australian dioceses could well take him on. I hate to see him losing his priestly vocation, as it were, because his conscience is pushing him into the Catholic Church.

A couple of weeks ago we buried old Father Sebastiaan Tromp, who wrote two encyclicals for Pius XII, acted as theologian for Cardinal Alfredo Ottaviani [the prefect of the Congregation for the Doctrine of the Faith], and did a great deal of work as theological secretary to the Second Vatican Council. The poor man saw many ideas endorsed that he found difficult to accept, as well as suffering from his own texts on revelation, scripture, and tradition being thrown out. But he took it patiently. On more than one occasion, he said: "after a good Scotch, I can accept any heresy." He really represents my theological grandfather here at the Gregorian, as I took over the course on revelation from René Latourelle, who took it over from Tromp.

From March 19, I will be away until April 7: in London, Cambridge, Oxford, and Tübingen. By the way Jock Harbison is not at all well; he is in intensive care and has, according to the latest report, a dangerous cancer. Eleanor might not want you or Moira to know. I would suggest not writing, but I thought it was well to let you and Moira know. My love to you all, Gerald.

Gregorian University, Rome, March 16, 1975.

My dear Mother, I was very glad you liked *Faith Under Fire*. My copies are still on the way. I know the content but don't yet know what the finished product looks like!

Pat Hayes, Eleanor's sister, lost her husband Tommy two weeks ago. He had suffered several heart attacks. So his death was not altogether unexpected. I had this news in a letter from Eleanor, who seems to be bearing up well through Jock's long sickness.

I did a piece in *The Tablet* on the past, present, and future of German Catholic theology, with a page towards the end on Hans Küng. On the way back from London I will stop a few days in Tübingen and may have a chat with him. I won't mention the article, unless he has already seen it and brings the matter up. Curiously there are probably hundreds or at least dozens of Catholics from Tübingen in Rome today— for the beatification of Fr Karl Steeb who was born there in the last century, founded a congregation of sisters, and died in Verona. I simply haven't had time to go looking for these Tübingener, although I'm sure some of them will be known to me. [Steeb founded the Sisters of Mercy of Verona, a religious institute which no longer exists.]

I hope *Has Dogma a Future?* will have reached you. Darton, Longman & Todd said they would send you a copy. Next Thursday I will get to London and go straight to have lunch with one of the directors, who leaves London that evening. It's so much easier to do business personally than via a letter.

I have booked a room for Maev in a pensione right under St Peter's for November 8–18. They were the dates she mentioned as fitting snugly into her sweep later in the year from Africa to England. As I said in an earlier letter, I leave here on March 20 and get back on April 7.

Much love and every blessing to you and the rest of the family for Easter, Gerald.

Gregorian University, Rome, April 13, 1975.

[This letter refers to Bill and Deirdre Athey (Deirdre being my first cousin), to Monica Ellison, another cousin and a younger sister of Eleanor Harbison, and to Joanna Peters, daughter of my sister Moira.]

My dear Mother, Stewart is enjoying himself in the eternal city—ten days at a pensione run by German nuns near St Peter's Square. In a few moments I am off to have lunch with him at a college for American priests doing graduate studies in Rome. On Wednesday (after he had been to a papal audience), we took a picnic lunch out at the Fosse Ardeatine, scene of a massacre during World War II and now an extremely moving memorial and museum.

England and Germany proved pretty cold over Easter. I came back by train via Bonn and Tübingen. Küng, unfortunately, was away; I had hoped to hear his reactions to the Roman document directed against him. In *The Tablet* for March 8, I did a piece on the present state of Catholic theology in the German-speaking world; the same issue carried a good article on the "Küng case."

Deirdre and Bill seemed very well and happy when I stayed with them for a night in London, as did Monica and John Ellison. No further news of Jock. I spoke to Eleanor on the phone. It's been a fearfully hard time for her, but she is bearing up with great courage. Harry, her eldest son, captained his team (Blackrock College) to an all-Ireland championship, winning the final on March 17 with his father struggling for life in hospital.

On Tuesday I head out of Rome to Nemi and give nine lectures to the Society of Divine Word tertians. [Tertians are priests or brothers in a religious institute engaged in a final year of spiritual formation.] Presumably there will be some there from Papua New Guinea. The group I spoke to before Christmas contained half a dozen from the New Guinea highlands. Nemi is a quiet, small town overlooking a stunning lake (of the same name). One can also look across the plains to the sea; clear air and skies make it a treat after the pollution in Rome.

Please congratulate Joanna on getting into London School of Economics; Stewart told me that. It will be great to see her in London next Christmas.

I am hard at the manuscript of *The Calvary Christ* in the hopes of finishing it before I leave Rome on May 31. I plan to make a brief stop in Dublin before heading on to Boston, and then eventually (around June 28) Dunedin. My love to you, Dympna, Jim [my brother], Posey [his wife], and all the family, Gerald.

Gregorian University, Rome, June 4, 1975.

[This letter refers to Ed and Jane Kirby and to Jim and Jacqueline McDonald, family friends who lived near New York.]

My dear Mother, After finishing classes in Rome last Saturday, I flew to Dublin for the weekend. [After Jock's death] Eleanor is bearing up well—with lots of courage and honesty. Jock's sister was down from Belfast, and we had a comforting Mass at home with the four youngsters contributing their own prayers of the faithful. It was sadly ironical that, just as Jock was dying, Harry was winning every rugby prize within reach, including playing for an all-Ireland team against England.

On Monday I flew to Boston and am now on the train for New York. I will see the Kirbys, the McDonalds, and others. The summer institute gets under way in Burlington, Vermont, on June 15, and, as soon as that finishes on June 21, I leave for Mosgiel in New Zealand. I expect to reach Melbourne around August 9.

I missed the big army parade in Rome on June 2, and yesterday's visit by President Gerald Ford to the Pope and to our next-door neighbour, the Italian President. [The Quirinal Palace, the home of the president, was right next door to the Gregorian University.]

Please wish Maev a very happy birthday on June 16, if you are on the phone to her [in Papua New Guinea]. Love, Gerald.

Holy Cross College, Mosgiel, July 20, 1975.

[This letter refers to Helder Camara, a saintly bishop from Brazil, and to Marion Peters, the eldest of my nieces.]

My dear Mother, Time is whistling by here on the South Island of New Zealand. Unkind critics, noting the drift to the North Island which set in after the gold rush days ended, remark: "Will the last person out of the South Island please switch off the lights." That's as bad as the instruction Rod McKuen quoted last night during his concert at the old Regent Theatre in Dunedin. "On the aircraft we were told: 'you are now approaching Auckland, New Zealand. Please set your watches back thirty years.'" All of that is hardly amusing, and is certainly unfair. People have been extraordinarily hospitable to me, and I appreciate the sense of dialogue which seems to operate at all levels of life.

Out here at Holy Cross I am giving twenty lectures (in Christology and fundamental theology) and about fifteen at Knox College, the Presbyterian establishment on the far side of the university campus. Then there are three open lectures at the University of Otago. Around fifty people came to last Thursday's first lecture in that series. We'll have to see whether the group grows or declines for next Thursday's lecture on "Jesus between Poetry and Philosophy."

Theologians seem to swarm regularly in New Zealand. Piet Fransen, a Belgium Jesuit, will be here shortly, as will Helder Camara. An Irish Dominican from Jerusalem, Jerry Murphy-

O'Connor, is to lecture in the North Island. On Monday—i.e. tomorrow—I will meet Monsignor Ralph Brown from the archdiocese of Westminster, who refused to give me an imprimatur for my dogma book last year. He is out in New Zealand lecturing on marriage tribunals. What do you say to a man who refused you an imprimatur?

There are about thirty seminarians at Holy Cross, many of them with good non-Catholic names like Wynn-Williams and Hay-Mackenzie. One of the staff explained it for me: "The girls stick to their Catholic faith [and pass it on] more than the boys." On his mother's side Wynn-Williams is a relative of Father Damien of Molokai [who ministered to lepers and is now canonized as St Joseph de Veuster].

There have been a few extras for me, like making a recording for the local radio. The interviewer asked one or two rather large questions, such as "What do you think is the difference between Christianity today and Christianity in the Middle Ages?"

I will be over in Melbourne late on the night of August 7, think of coming down to Frankston [a suburb where my Mother lived] for the weekend, and have suggested to Marion that she might come also. I will give you a call and find out about arrangements on August 8. Love to you and the rest of the family at Frankston, Gerald.

Gregorian University, Rome, September 27, 1975.

My dear Mother, As my typewriter is being serviced, I hope you won't mind this scrawl of mine. Thanks for your letter from Bunns Springs [the farm in South Australia run by my sister Moira and her husband Jim]. It made me happy that you were back there—the surest sign of recovered vigour.

I wrote a piece on the Papua New Guinea independence celebrations for *The Tablet*, but have not yet heard whether they will print it. [They did not.] At present, time is taken up with the usual pre-year chores: preparing bibliographies, making course outlines etc.

Archbishop Frank Little [of Melbourne] seemed to have enjoyed his four weeks in Rome—at a theological consultation with nearly thirty US bishops. I had dinner with him on Thursday evening. Tomorrow I go to the Scots College and lecture for a group of Glasgow priests. Normally they [the seminarians of the Scots College] are supposed to be back by October 1.

A very happy birthday on October 5, provided this letter reaches you in time. My love to all the family, Gerald.

Gregorian University, Rome, October 20, 1975.

[This letter refers to my nephew Stewart Peters and to Marie O'Connor, the mother of my cousins Eleanor, Pat, Monica, Bobby, and Paul.]

My dear Mother, I was glad to hear that Denis Kirby [son of Ed and Jane] made it to Australia. Earlier this year, Ed told me that he might do so. It should encourage Ed and Jane to come themselves when Ed retires in a couple of years time.

The warm weather faded out a week ago, and classes started for me today. Around 130 in a course on fundamental theology. John and Judy Brophy [from Sydney], friends of Maev, were here in Rome last week. On Friday they took me out to see the Etruscan tombs in Tarquinia and a nearby necropolis. Fascinating, especially as we had a good guide.

Moltmann and another German theologian friend of mine [Josef Nolte] were in Rome last week for a congress on the theology of the cross. One evening I brought Moltmann to dinner at the North American College. He gave an informal talk to the students, and then yarned nearly till midnight with Cardinal Medeiros of Boston. The Cardinal was a bit surprised to hear what was said about the Eucharist and inter-communion, but took it well, and warmly invited Moltmann to stay with him next time he visits Boston.

I am wondering whether my piece on Papua New Guinea got to *The Tablet* or was lost in the mail. Normally I would have received a quick letter from Tom Burns [the editor], but none has come.

Darton, Longman & Todd received the manuscript of *The Calvary Christ* last month. Soon enough I will hear from them. They seemed interested. So I presume they will take it. [They didn't; in the UK, SCM Press published the book.] But they didn't commit themselves to a date of publication. It might be as late as next May or even June.

I dashed off a letter to Stewart yesterday, to make sure we meet up in December. I will be in London December 19–23, before giving a retreat in Worcester.

Marie O'Connor died last month, as you may have heard. Monica Ellison wrote last week to give me the news. Marie was sick for only a few days. It was a great comfort to her to have Pat, Monica, Bobby, Paul, and other members of the family there.

Not much other news. This year I am getting my tongue

around Italian a bit better, but still have a fair way to go. Much love, Gerald.

Gregorian University, Rome, November 9, 1975.

[This letter refers to Bobby, another Irish cousin. She lived in Wexford with her mother Marie, who had saved many letters from my grandfather, Patrick McMahon Glynn, and had years before sent them to me.]

My dear Mother, Thank you for the letter from last month and the cable. In fact, Marie didn't save any more letters [than the ones I had already received], but only a few documents. I have written to Eleanor (who is often in Wexford) to say that I would be delighted to have any documents or papers in danger of being thrown out. But there really isn't much there, except for the life of grandfather's mother written by Aunt Agnes. And I doubt whether Bobby would throw that out. So not to worry.

That is awfully good of you to think of putting $1,000 towards the project of "likely" people teaching here at the Gregorian. In fact, the dean seems pleased to go along with the project. Maybe Dympna could have a special account for holding the money? Whatever happens, the Gregorian needs new blood. One way of getting such new blood is to invite visiting lecturers, who prove themselves and then can be asked to stay permanently. But the initial step is to find money for fares etc and get them here in the first place as visitors. Your contribution will be more than welcome. I will let you know what turns up. At present the dean of theology is planning courses and professors for 1976/77.

Maev seems well, and is doing a bit of work (putting together lectures) between sightseeing and some shopping. She leaves for Libya on Thursday, and returns ten days later for a short stay before going on to London.

I still haven't heard from *The Tablet*. But *America* magazine accepted a piece I did on the imagination of Jesus. That should appear around Christmas.

On Friday the weather finally turned bad, and the swallows arrived to gather for their flight back to Africa. Last night I finally had a meal at the Capranica, a fifteenth-century seminary that sends students to the Gregorian. The original building is lovely, even if renovated. Pius XII was one of their students. I have been trying to visit all the seminaries and colleges that provide us with students, but there is a large number of them. Much love, Gerald.

Gregorian University, Rome, December 7, 1975.

[The letter refers to a visit of my sister Dympna and two of her children, and to the imminent Australian federal election held on December 13, when Malcolm Fraser won a landslide victory over Gough Whitlam.]

My dear Mother, Although this mightn't reach you till after Christmas, a very happy Christmas and New Year. John Reilly, an Australian Jesuit who has been staying at the Gregorian for a couple of months, heads home in a couple of days, and I will ask him to post this and other letters when he reaches Melbourne.

I hope that the arrangements for Dymps & Co. turn out OK. Several friends have offered to look after them. Unfortunately,

I leave for London, to work in a parish and lead a retreat, the day before she arrives. But I will see her in January when she returns to Rome before flying home.

December 8, letter resumed. This morning the Pope celebrates the 10 o'clock Mass in St Peter's, to which all the faculty members and students of papal universities and athenaeums in Rome have been invited. The story is that a special, papal document is expected today, the tenth anniversary of the closing of Vatican II. [*Evangelii Nuntiandi* (Announcing the Gospel), an apostolic exhortation on evangelization, was in fact issued that day.]

Thursday next, Qantas is holding a surprise party for all Australians in Rome, with special pies flown in from Sydney and so forth. Whose plot to gain votes is this? Did Gough Whitlam [Prime Minister of Australia 1972–75] prepare this last year—or was it earlier in this year?—when he visited Rome? Or is Malcolm Fraser [elected Prime Minister in December 1975] behind it all? At any rate we will all be there to clutch our Foster's beer and swallow our pies.

I fly over to London on December 19, lead a retreat, have an evening or two with Stewart, do some business, and get back to Rome on January 4. I will see Darton, Longman & Todd in London. It looks as if they and Paulist Press (in New York) will publish *The Calvary Christ*. [In fact, SCM Press published the book in the UK, and Westminster Press did so in the USA.]

We have settled down to the regular Roman winter—cool nights and days of sunshine. With luck this weather could last until early February. Much love for Christmas and the New Year, Gerald.

Gregorian University, Rome, January 11, 1976.

[This letter refers to Jamie, my brother Jim's son, to Jim's sister-in-law, Katherine Calder, and her daughters, to John and Monica Ellison, and to cousin Deirdre, married to Bill Athey.]

My dear Mother, Thank you for the two letters and, of course, the greetings from Jamie. From this distance it sounds good if he can attend catechism classes and prepare to receive Holy Communion. In England I picked up a couple of little books for Gigi Mason—home from boarding school and, as Katie told me, also keen to make her first Communion.

In London I saw Katie and the three girls a couple of times—once, in fact, on Christmas Day. Everyone seemed well and happy. I dashed around there [Chelsea] after helping to serve dinner and then have dinner myself at Providence Row where I was staying. It's a refuge for homeless people, both married and single, near Liverpool Street Railway Station. It has been in operation for a hundred years or more. Not far away is the Jack the Ripper Pub, right opposite a graceful, Christopher Wren-style, Anglican church. J. the R. "operated" in that part of London, and one of his victims was a woman who was or had been staying at Providence Row. These days the sad (or sinister?) people staying there are those from Northern Ireland. Several girls from Belfast were at the dinner. After arriving a few days earlier in London, they had been held and questioned by the police, and seemed to be still under surveillance. A stately gentleman with a firm moustache served the beer. He turned out to a gentleman in waiting to the late Cardinal Heenan. His family has always sent someone to help with the Christmas dinner at Providence Row, for as long as anyone can remember.

In London, I spent half a day with Stewart [Peters], stayed with the Ellisons (and said Mass for them at home), saw Deirdre and Bill Athey briefly, and got a bit of business done with Robin Baird-Smith, a director of Darton, Longman & Todd. Then brief stops in Oxford and Cambridge, before giving a retreat in Worcester for about thirty sisters.

The "hurricane" arrived during one evening conference and brought down the weather cock on the house. In Worcester three or four people died, and nearly thirty in the whole country. It was all over in about thirty minutes, but the wind really blew hard then.

During my absence, Dympna seems to have met all and sundry here in Rome, and returns around Wednesday of this week. It's a bit unclear; at any rate the accommodation is there for her and the two boys. A couple of seminarians, a priest, and several sisters I know looked after the three of them in various ways.

Nine more class days for me, and then the exams (about fifty oral and twenty-five written exams). The second semester gets off the ground about February 15.

Please wish Jim [my brother] a happy birthday from me, retrospectively. I forgot to include birthday greetings in my Christmas letter. Both Stewart and I lamented INTENSELY that we couldn't be with Jim on election night, and we promise—yes, Jim, we promise—to make up for your absence by a replay of that evening with you just as soon as possible. Love, Gerald. [The reference is to the landslide victory Malcolm Fraser won in the national election in Australia on December 13, after Gough Whitlam had served as Prime Minister (1972–75).]

Gregorian University, Rome, February 7, 1976.

[This letter refers to Ellie, a daughter of my brother Glynn.]

My dear Mother, This letter comes fairly hard on the heels of the return of Dympna and her children. They must have given you much of the news from the Roman front. One thing Dymps may not have mentioned was her—once again!—sensing things at a distance. When she got back to Rome in January, she asked me: "Is anyone sick or dead?" "No," I said. "I've just had a letter from Moira and all seems well." And then a day or two later a letter came telling Dymps that the father of Sue [her daughter-in-law] was dying. Another example of Dymps's powers!

While the rest of Europe, or at least northern Europe, has been shivering in sub-freezing weather, we bask down here in our sunshine. I enjoy noting in the daily paper how the temperature in Rome can be ten, fifteen, or even twenty degrees above that in London.

Exams start on Monday and continue for several days. Then on Tuesday week the second semester gets under way. This coming semester, besides the ordinary commitments, I have taken on an evening course in Italian to lay people from Rome who enrol in their hundreds at the Gregorian for courses in theology and philosophy. Teaching them may help, incidentally, to improve my Italian. One gets along in a kind of modified Italian with many of the ordinary, seminary students, who may be Spaniards, Africans, or what have you.

Please wish Ellie a happy birthday from on February 22. Will she be nine then?

I have just come from talking with a Spanish Jesuit about putting out a Spanish translation of *The Easter Jesus*. It seems likely, although one can never tell. [In the event, the book did not have a Spanish translation.]

Much love to all the family, Gerald. PS I am getting this letter back to Australia via a priest returning from Rome.

Gregorian University, Rome, February 25, 1976.

My dear Mother, The days are turning longer at a good pace. We have a new government, and a few visitors are arriving. Yesterday Jim McDonald, an American lawyer, phoned and we had dinner together at L'Eau Vive, a restaurant run by religious sisters from a large number of countries. They wear their own national dress. The restaurant is unique, being the only one in Rome where women serve. Most of the time you can't get near the place for parliamentarians and clerics. Jim is over here trying to sort out some matters concerned with multinationals bribing Italians. He is not representing Lockheed but some other interests. [Bribes made by Lockheed to negotiate the sale of aircraft around the world were beginning to have political repercussions. In June 1978, the President of Italy, Giovanni Leone, was to resign.]

Last Saturday I finally got to see the Collegium Teutonicum ad Campum Sanctum. I have two Irish (student) friends living there, but just about everyone else is German. The college perches between St Peter's Basilica and the papal audience hall—right inside the Vatican. You enter through a cemetery, at which archaeologists seem to be ever probing away. The traditional place of St Peter's martyrdom lies just outside the gate. That's also the place from which the obelisk was shifted to its present position in front of the basilica [and out in St Peter's Square].

After a drink, we went off to eat at a German restaurant, where a cassocked, German-speaking (Swiss) monsignor, who was doing "nicely, nicely," presided over a *Stammtisch* [reserved table] for half a dozen Swiss guards. No one seemed to take the slightest notice of the monsignor, a large man in a well-buttoned cassock, with his flat, black hat hanging nearby. That appears to be the place to find the Swiss guards on their nights off. It certainly demythologized matters to see them out of their uniforms.

Not too much other news. I had one of my annual lunches with Fr Jean Leclercq, a tremendously travelled Benedictine who, this year, for instance, lectures in Rome, the United States (twice), Australia and, I think, Luxembourg. They are always a superb swopping of news and views—those lunches of ours.

Please wish Francis [my brother Glynn's eldest child] a very happy birthday from me.

It's a hopelessly busy term this one. It has made me do something that I have never done before—prescribe a textbook, in this case *Il Gesù pasquale*, the Italian translation of [my] *The Easter Jesus*. That's for an evening course, two hours a week with 25 to 30 Italians, laity and religious. Much love to you all, Gerald.

Gregorian University, Rome, April 1, 1976.

[This letter refers to Sister Margaret Treacy whose ministry in leading retreats I tried to support.]

My dear Mother, A very happy Easter to you and the rest of the family. Thank you very much indeed for the money for the library here at the Gregorian, as well as support for Sister

Margaret. Both gifts will do a great deal of good. Our theology section needs a bit of sprucing up in the English-language section, for the sake of the English-speaking students who run to over 30%.

Last Thursday I tried to beat the strike by getting a bus out of Rome to the Castelli Romani at 8.45. But the bus company, which serves the runs from Rome to the Castelli and provides an excellent, cheap service, had decided to join the general strike fifteen minutes early. So there was nothing to do but wait until eleven o'clock when the general strike, Italian-style, was over. Divine providence, however, intervened in the person of a student from Cambridge who became a don at Oxford and is now studying for the priesthood at the English College. He suddenly appeared with a car and ran me out to their villa. In the grounds of the villa a consul's tomb recalls the imperial past. The place was a monastery during the Middle Ages, and a barracks for German soldiers during World War II. The Germans left behind some fine drawings in the dining room—in the form of coats of arms on the walls. We drank champagne to celebrate the installation of the new Archbishop of Westminster [Basil Hume], and ate the lunch provided by the Italian lady who lives at the villa with her family.

In a few minutes I am off to do my first Vatican Radio broadcast: on Christ's resurrection. At the moment the Vatican and the Paul VI himself could do with a few resurrections. The Pope has issued a ukase against non-Catholics teaching at the Gregorian and other Catholic universities and colleges in Rome. Highly embarrassing, as non-Catholic theologians have been coming as visiting professors for eight years or so. Last week Pope Paul received in private audience the very

Anglican the Gregorian has invited to teach again next year, Harry Smythe, an Australian who heads the Anglican Centre in Rome. Harry was delivering a letter from Dr Michael Ramsey, thanking the Pope for the meeting ten years ago which led to much closer collaboration between Rome and Canterbury. Harry doesn't know the bad news yet. Perhaps the rector of the Gregorian may be able to reverse the papal decision. Of course, one is never sure from how high up such decisions come. But in this case Vatican officials like Cardinal Garrone [Prefect of the Congregation for Catholic Education and ex ufficio chancellor of the Gregorian] are denying that it is their decision.

Next week I head off to make a retreat and get back to Rome from Villa Cavalletti (at Frascati) just before Easter Sunday. Love, Gerald.

Gregorian University, Rome, May 9, 1976.

[This letter refers to Mother Paul, a Dominican teacher of my Mother, to Michael and Lu Linton, the younger sister of Posey, my sister-in-law, and to my niece Marion.]

My dear Mother, I was glad you heard my Easter broadcast on Vatican Radio. How on earth did you all know it was on? When I made the recording here in Rome, I never thought to ask whether the program would be heard in Australia.

I have just come from a prayer meeting where I met again a couple of Dominican sisters from North Adelaide. Just last Thursday I ran into them for the first time; they are right at the end of a year's course in Rome. We had plenty to talk about— Mother Paul, you, and your generation. By sheer coincidence they are going to be at a Mass I am saying next Thursday for an Australian family who are about to leave Rome. A case of maximum exposure to people in minimum time!

A party of 25 Swedish students from the University of Lund are in Rome at present, on a week of visiting with one of their professors. On Friday night the Jesuit students at the International College of the Gesù entertained them: a prayer service, supper, and a sing song. On Tuesday the Swedes will attend my lectures on Christ's death and resurrection, or rather an hour's lecture followed by discussion. I hope some of my students will pitch in and show them around the Gregorian, after the two periods of academic exercising are over.

Please tell Michael and Lu how very greatly I enjoyed their visit, with their two friends. It was an evening of utterly relaxed good fun being together.

Next week the theology faculty elects its dean for the next triennium. There is really only one feasible candidate, a French-Canadian, 44 years of age, who has been teaching at the University of Montreal [Gilles Pelland]. Some of the old guard think he is too young! Poor Jesus could never have served as dean here, not to mention a number of other things for which he would have been too young. Thank God there was no age limit for saving the world, or else we would all be still in trouble.

I am trying to get as much work out of the way before the arrivals [some of my family] from Melbourne show up. Class unfortunately goes on till May 26, and then there are exams & essays to correct. But skilful planning can get some days free for the gang.

SCM Press has accepted *The Calvary Christ*. I asked them to let me have a contract at once to make sure that nothing goes astray this time. The editor spoke about getting the book out in time for the Lent of next year. Love to all the family. PS Please give a special "Hi" from me to Marion [Peters] and wish her well in the exams.

As from 48 Lexington Avenue, Cambridge, Mass. 02138, July 12, 1976.

[This letter refers to Jim McDonald, a lawyer already mentioned in my letter of February 25, 1976.]

My dear Mother, I left Rome on June 19 with a "good omen," in that Mother Teresa of Calcutta was on the flight to New York. We chatted about various things, including her good effect on Malcolm Muggeridge, whose latest book sees him arriving at full faith in Christ. I will see her again in Philadelphia at the Eucharistic Congress in August. Jim and Jackie McDonald were out at Kennedy airport to pick me up. They were sorry to have just missed Mother Teresa, but then on the run into the city we drew alongside the car carrying Mother Teresa and they joined in my big wave to her. I spent several days at Wyckoff with the McDonalds, sleeping late and generally recovering from the last hectic days in Rome. Mark, their son who begins an engineering course at Duke University, took me into New York for the latest Neil Simon play, *California Suite*.

From New York I caught the train north to New Haven and Yale, where, sad to say, I found my young friends, George and Sue Hunsinger, had just been divorced. All in all, it wasn't as hard as last year, at least not as emotionally painful when I visited them and tried to save the situation. Then Ed and Jane Kirby picked me up and we drove to Springfield, Massachusetts, to spend the night with Ed's brother, Al Kirby. The next day Ed and Jane dropped me in Cambridge, Massachusetts en route to a reunion of US Marines in New Hampshire. Bernd Stappert, a friend of mine from Stuttgart, was in town, just at the end of three weeks in the States, during which he was interviewing right and left: Kenneth Galbraith, Harvey Cox, and other academics.

Then on June 27 I came up to Winooski and began work at a summer school in religious education. Two 75-minute periods a day and 40 in the class make the days pretty strenuous. But they are most agreeable people, nearly all of them teachers or coordinators of Christian doctrine programs in parishes. Last weekend I dropped down to Middlebury to see Myron Magnet and his wife. Myron was with me at Pembroke College. On July 4, we joined most of the other Middleburyans at a barbecue lunch on the village green. That long weekend I also got up to Stowe and the chalet run by Maria von Trapp.

Yesterday four of us drove down to Weston Priory for Mass. There fifteen Benedictines have a fascinating, new-style monastery. You must have heard their music. At present they are cutting a new record. At Mass I caught sight of a familiar face and thought: "that can't be Russell Roide. He is teaching at a Jesuit high school in San Francisco." But indeed it was he, a former student of mine from Weston School of Theology in Cambridge, Mass. Russell was at the priory making a retreat.

I suppose some of the travellers are back by now? Next Friday I go south to the above address, and that will be my base until I leave for London on 22 August. Much love, Gerald.

As from 48 Lexington Avenue, Cambridge, Mass., July 31, 1976.

My dear Mother, On July 17, I took a leisurely bus ride from Middlebury (Vermont) down through the lovely, New England forests to Boston. Lots of good things in the greater Boston area this summer. On Sunday evening, July 18, several thousand of us watched ballet on the Cambridge Common. Later that week I saw a rather challenging, multimedia show on the past, present, and future of the city, "Where's Boston?" That was held in a pavilion at the Prudential Center. Afterwards I wandered off to look at the vast headquarters and mother church of Christian Science. The buildings are grouped together around a small lake with great beds of flowers lining the water.

Last Monday, I went up to Marblehead to visit Dennis Sheehan, a priest I worked with in Rome. Jim, Moira, and other members of our family have met him. To end the visit to Dennis, I went on to Rockport, a delightful fishing village before heading back to Boston.

At the moment I am in New York, en route to speak at the Eucharistic Congress in Philadelphia. I will be back in Cambridge, Mass., and leave from there on August 23. My address in London (August 23–September 8) is Convent of Mercy, 50 Crispin Street, London E1 6HQ). Much love, Gerald.

As from Gregorian University, Rome, August 23, 1976.

My dear Mother, It was a delight to receive your letter with all its news. I wrote to Marion [Peters] to congratulate her [on passing examinations for the first part of her fellowship in the Royal Australian College of Physicians] and encourage her to think of further work in Europe. Talking of travel and plans, I will fly from Rome to San Francisco to teach in a summer school during July 1977. After that, I can return to Rome via Australia.

En route to the Eucharistic Congress in Philadelphia, I stopped in New York to have dinner with Paul and Heidrun Rotterdam, friends from Cambridge, Mass. They have a floor of a century-old factory down near Canal Street in lower Manhattan. On the other floors are some other painters and a poet (who perhaps needs a lot of space to write?). Heidrun works as a pathologist at the Lennox Hill Hospital; Paul teaches part-time at Harvard in the fine arts department, and paints. He's the only person I have ever heard of to get tenure at Harvard, although he's there two/three days a week for only one semester. Harvard supplies him with a suite of rooms in Adams House. The Museum of Modern Art in Paris has just bought one of his paintings, people are writing articles on his work, and in lots of ways he's arrived. By the way, if you ever run into Patrick McCaughey [Professor of Fine Arts at Monash University, Melbourne], please mention Paul's name. Patrick must know his work. Maybe Patrick could arrange a lecturing visit to Australia? Paul has his PhD from Vienna and, as I said, is a tenured professor at the Carpenter Center in Harvard. I know Paul would be glad to have such an invitation, if only to see his sister, married and living in Sydney.

In Philadelphia I stopped at the Bellevue Stratford Hotel, the headquarters for a meeting of the American Legion in late July. Twenty-six people caught some mysterious complaint and died, nearly all legionnaires. My theory is that a mysterious toilet-blocker (whom the assistant manager told me about) switched to poisoning people. The doctors have ruled out viruses and diseases of various sorts. [In fact, they were to identify something new, a severe form of pneumonia caused by the Legionella bacteria and called the Legionnaires Disease.] The story about the deaths started coming out during the last days of the Congress. As I left the hotel, a girl from a local radio station interviewed me and asked: "How did you feel about staying in a hotel which was the center of the disease?" "I've lived in much less healthy countries than the United States," I told her.

In the London *Tablet* for August 14, you can read my impressions of the Congress. I left out one major difference between the '73 Congress in Melbourne and the Congress in Philadelphia: no horse race meeting like the one at Flemington. Remember the Congress Stakes? In Philadelphia I saw Archbishop Little and Bishop Perkins [Australians, from Melbourne], who filled me in with lots of news. Avery Dulles was there too, and we engaged in one of our enormously long theological discussions. He may be in Rome during 1977, on a Woodrow Wilson Fellowship.

On the way back from Philadelphia I stopped with the Kirbys at Normandy Beach (New Jersey shore), took a ride in a launch with Ed and the rest. Before returning to Cambridge, Mass., I stayed (to say Mass and give one talk) at Marymount in Tarrytown-on-Hudson. Nelson Rockefeller lives just across the hill. Every day his helicopter was buzzing up and down the Hudson valley. Just outside his back gate was a grassy area where a Mercy convent had been. He bought the property, and demolished the building. To improve his view? Nearby is the home of Washington Irving, Sunnyside, a lovely house on the banks of the river. The old lady who met me at the door proudly showed off the rooms, especially the study:

"Mr Irving's publishers, Putnams. gave him that desk. They are still in business in New York." The way she spoke of "Mr Irving," I expected him to come around the corner and take over the job of tour guide.

Please give Jim and Posey, Jamie and Tori [the children of Jim and Posey], etc. my love, and pass on this letter around the "compound" [the family houses which were close together at Frankston]. Tomorrow I leave for two days in Ireland and a retreat (to lead) in London. Love, Gerald.

London, September 4, 1976.

My dear Mother, Last night I had dinner with Joanna [Peters], and we chatted on till midnight. She seems on top of things for her exams which begin next Tuesday [in international law at London School of Economics]. I had just finished giving a retreat to twenty Mercy sisters—with the help of Sr Margaret Treacy, who was a tremendous assistance.

That is very kind of Posey to suggest that I come out at Christmas. I am pretty sure I can say yes. Please thank Posey for the generous invitation. So, as soon as I get back to Rome (around September 29), I will make a booking and let you know the details. It could only be for two weeks, as I teach up to about December 22 and then start again on January 7.

Kerry looked beautiful when I stopped two days with Eleanor [Harbison] and the kids. Tony, the younger son, took me fishing, and then Eleanor ran me up to Cork for a flight to London.

Love to all the family, and let Posey know that almost certainly my visit will be OK. Love, Gerald. PS I will give Katie [Posey's sister in London] a call this weekend.

Gregorian University, Rome, October 7, 1976

My dear Mother, I was very sorry to forget to write to you for your birthday. Please put it down to the rush of getting back to Rome from Germany. Anyway accept my love and best wishes, retrospectively. Please pass on my greetings to Jim Peters [brother-in-law] and Tori [O'Collins, niece] on October 20.

The twelve days in Germany flew past. I stayed with some old friends (Josef and Ingrid Nolte) in their house in Hirschau, a village about three miles up the Neckar from Tübingen. From being a village of about 500 inhabitants a decade back, Hirschau has grown to about 3,000—many of them young couples like Josef and Ingrid. Loads of children, flowers and gardens everywhere. Behind their house runs a ridge with vineyards clinging to the slopes. The grape harvest began just at the end of my stay. Blue nets had been covering the grapes, although there weren't many birds to be seen—normally just three buzzards circling high above the ridge. This runs from Tübingen to a famous old chapel, the Wurmlinger Kapelle (from the 12th century). When I was there one Sunday, I saw six statues of Our Lady lining the walls, lovely pieces of art from the medieval period and later. The oldest object in the chapel was, I think, a solemn-faced Christ astride a donkey— for the Palm Sunday procession.

Moltmann was away (in the United States) and so too was Küng (home in Switzerland). I saw that Küng had prescribed, for the students taking a course with him in 1976/77, his *Twenty Theses*, a summary of his big work, *On Being a Christian*, which appears any day now in English translation.

I went with Josef Nolte for a day in Munich. It happened to be the opening day of the Oktoberfest. But Josef was at a meeting, preparing nine radio discussions that he and some other Germans are to make in Rome shortly. After lunch with the group and suggesting that they contact Gore Vidal in Rome, I went off to the Alte Pinakotek. They intend to include some interviews in the broadcasts: for instance, an interview with the new (Communist) mayor of Rome.

When I left Josef & Ingrid, I managed to do something I had never done before. I caught the wrong train. In Stuttgart I went to the right platform, but boarded a train going north to Nuremberg and not south to Constance. It turned out to be a special, a *Sonderzug*, pulled by a steam engine plus diesel (just in case!). It blew the mind of the conductor that anyone could catch the wrong train; I fell right outside the categories he lived and worked by. So I had a free ride to Nuremberg. Karl Holzbauer, a priest friend of mine, lives very close to the railway station. I stopped with him for the weekend before taking a train to Munich and then to Rome. Karl runs Caritas [an organization for social services] in Nuremberg; his job takes him to Northern Ireland, Beirut, India etc.—all places where he dispenses relief.

Everything is fixed up for Christmas. I have booked on Qantas to get me to Melbourne on December 23. I guess the ticket has been paid for now at the Melbourne end. I will give the Rome office a call tomorrow to check reservations. Love to all the family, Gerald.

Gregorian University, Rome, October 31, 1976.

My dear Mother,

Two weeks into term here, and I am glad to have the break over this weekend, a *ponte*, as the Italians call it. Monday and Tuesday (November 1 and 2) are holidays. The government has abolished a number of holidays and *ponti*, and I dare say the Gregorian will have to follow suit next year. Warm and wet here, instead of the usual October weather—of sunny days and cooler evenings.

Last week I sent back to the SCM Press the corrected proofs of *The Calvary Christ*. The book is due out on February 1. A group of German friends were in town till yesterday, making nine radio broadcasts on life (past and present) in Rome. Not much other news. These days are taken up with students and their needs. One just dropped by to chat about his courses, before taking a visitor to see the Roman Forum.

I will write soon. Please wish James and Stephen Peters [two nephews] a happy birthday from me. Love, Gerald.

Gregorian University, Rome, January 16, 1977.

My dear Mother, I hope you don't mind if I ask you to send on this letter to Jim and Posey, Dympna & Dominic, Jim & Moira, Stewart & Marion, and Maev, if necessary. (Maev, are you still there at Glynneath?). Is this a chain letter I am committing? If so, so be it, and please pass it on, and to anyone else in the family who would like a read.

It goes without saying how deeply moving it was to see you all again, share Maev's operation, give James his First

Communion, baptize Eliza [a niece of Posey], and catch up a little on all the living that has been done these last fifteen months. Thanks for making Christmas for me in Melbourne possible. I felt there was so little time, so much not said, and so many conversations rushed to an end. But the love was there, and I came back to Rome with the loving presence of all of you ever so vivid. I felt just deeply happy to see you all again, and in a special way the children. I hate to miss anything of the adventure of their growing up.

Our flight had a couple of swoops at Tehran airport, finally gave it up as a bad job because of the snow & mist, and took us off to Bahrein. When I got back to the Gregorian, most of the community—or at least those who had been away for Christmas—were home, except my neighbour, a Polish canonist [Anton Mruk]. He'll be back shortly. Given what he went through (first Auschwitz and then Dachau after being arrested in November 1939), he is a stunningly happy man. [Eventually, Mruk became confessor to Pope John Paul II.]

Life caught up with me as soon as I returned: correcting the proofs of *What are they saying about Jesus?* (what indeed, sir?), meeting Fergus McCann (a Marist brother from Fribourg), saying a farewell Mass for Ruth Schwalenberg (a mother general off to spend six weeks in Uganda visiting the houses of her congregation), wondering how to translate a passage from St Gregory the Great into Italian ("the Scriptures provide waters in which lambs may walk and elephants may swim"), and reading pages and pages of theses. Next week a Miami priest [Vincent Malatesta] defends his thesis on the cosmology of purgatory in French preaching from the 16th to the 19th century. How about that for a topic of burning interest?

Yesterday we celebrated, first with a Mass at the Gesù and then with a reception here at the Gregorian, the fifty years of Father Pedro Arrupe in the Society of Jesus. A modern saint, if ever I met one, he preached an astonishingly fine sermon. My critical eye couldn't help noticing that only one Vatican bishop came, an excellent Spaniard who runs the Secretariat for Christian Unity. He is supposed to have been suspended years ago from his priestly functions, because of activities in Spain for youth. I'm not sure whether it's true, but he's certainly the only bishop I have ever met about whom I have heard such a story. He's the kind of person about whom it could be true. At the Vatican they are not *all* worldly compromisers. It's a pity that some of these worldly compromisers didn't come, to show a bit of human respect for Fr Arrupe, instead of the petty persecution that he puts up with from some of them.

Classes resumed, of course, last week. Term ends next week. Then February hits us with the exams. I have ten hours of orals. The students have a choice in any given subject—of doing an oral or a written exam. There must be a tradition among them that I am a softer option in an oral. At any rate, practically all of them have chosen the oral with me.

Happy wedding anniversary to Leslie [a nephew] and Sue on the 19th [January]. to Glynn and Steph on the 21st (their 13th!), and a happy birthday to Stewart [oldest nephew] on the 3rd [February]. LIFE BEGINS AT THIRTY, Stew. I give up with all the other birthdays.

Maev, I forgot to give you the address: Paulist Press, 400 Sette Drive, Paramus, New Jersey 07652. I think that's the right address; it's certainly a branch of the Paulist Press. The China book, a paperback [*The New China: A Catholic Response*, which I edited], comes out next week.

For those who know him, I haven't seen Dennis [Sheehan] yet. Last week he got back from Christmas with his brother and sister. These days there's a nice smell of roasted chestnuts in the streets, even if the weather remains warmish and wet.

And that's about all the news from the banks of the old Tiber. Much love to all of you, a big hug to all the children, and hurry over just as soon as you can, Gerald.

Gregorian University, Rome, February 3, 1977.

[This was the last letter my Mother received from me before her death.]

My dear Mother, I hope I didn't act as the importer of that flu which you had to put up with. Great to hear about your 1977 target; it has the support of my prayers.

Today was full of sunshine—with the dirigible carrying a big ad for Goodyear wandering around above Rome. I went out to have lunch at the Beda College with a couple of the faculty and ran into an Australian nun (from Wangaratta) who belongs to the convent attached to the Beda. In a few minutes I am off to have an Indian meal with Ravi Santosh Kamath, the Indian who sent you the card. He defends his thesis on February 12.

Monica Ellison sends her love to you and the others she knows in the family. Jane [her eldest daughter] has been accepted at Newnham College, Cambridge, and won a scholarship. The Ellisons were all very happy over that. When I am over [in London] at Easter, I may miss Jane, as she doesn't start till October and will fill in the months doing something abroad. I think she has a chance of working for a radio station in Cologne.

Last Monday classes ended for the first semester. The group I was teaching wanted to spend the last session discussing the document against women's ordination [*Inter Insigniores*, a declaration from the Congregation for the Doctrine of the Faith, dated October 15, 1976 but published only on January 27, 1977]. The final author [Eduard Dhanis] of the document lives at the Gregorian! The text is so weak, scripturally and, to some extent, theologically, I almost felt like writing a version which would improve the arguments for the status quo.

Jamie's Corner. Jamie [a nephew], thank you for your note. I look forward to seeing [your sketch of] "the twelve days of Christmas." I hope you have been able to mend the chain and can wear that medal by now. [From Rome I had brought him a medal for his First Communion at Christmas.]

Copies of *The Calvary Christ* are on their way to you from London and should arrive early next month. I doubt if the book will be on sale in Australia much before Easter.

At the Beda, incidentally, I met a New Zealander who will be ordained next summer for the Westminster Archdiocese. He is a jockey and, during his studies in Rome, has ridden for one or more Italian stables. You get used to meeting lawyers, ex-military people etc. at the Beda. But a jockey, I think, must be a first. My love to all, Gerald.

Part II:
The Coming of Pope John Paul II
(1978–1994)

Gregorian University, Rome, October 12, 1978.

[This letter refers to my sister-in-law, Posey.]

> My dear Maev, A friend is flying out to Australia in a day or so; hence this letter. Thanks awfully for the books and for the money for the Dean of Pembroke College, Cambridge. At the Gregorian, that edition of the *Summa Theologiae* will be much appreciated and long remain the standard work. [I referred to the gift of all 61 volumes of the translation prepared by Thomas Gilby, OP, and others.]

> *Epoca*, a glossy weekly from Milan, carried much of what I said to Desmond O'Grady over the phone. The new rector here, Carlo Martini, liked the piece—which cheered me greatly, as I am never sure of the ins and outs of Italian church politics, even when you want to say nice things about a lovely pope who has just died [John Paul I]. Someone carried a copy off to Posey in Melbourne. You can try out your Italian, or rather sample my Italian.

The cardinals better elect a successor to John Paul by Sunday or Monday. Otherwise when I give my first class on Tuesday, I won't have a soul there. Watch Cardinal Giovanni Benelli! The sense around town seems to be that you need a man with a gigantic and proven capacity to handle the work on Vatican Hill. Or is the choice between a loving, charismatic, communicative person who can't take the stress [another John Paul I] and an efficient bureaucrat? At any rate it seems clear that the cardinals may shift their criteria this time. I hope they will realize they picked a winner and look again for a good pastor. To hell with the work! The Vatican would be far better off, if it was all scaled down and the dioceses could handle their own affairs. Parkinson's Law operates like fury there, or probably several of Parkinson's laws.

I am off to have a pizza with Dennis Sheehan. I am sure he would send his love to you all if he knew I was writing this letter.

The Germans and Austrians got ordained this week in San Ignazio—all seven of them. A tremendous choir from Münster cathedral. A full church with the Germans lifting the roof off. It all acts like a great cathedral for me. The Hungarian primate (a cardinal) did the ceremony and preached at length, starting from the Turkish occupation of Hungary and ending with Pope John Paul saying the rosary. [Allegedly John Paul I died saying the rosary.] But his sermon fell short of the length of yesterday's first Mass of one of my students, or rather the sermon preached by the lad's parish priest. A good forty minutes. Or rather a bad forty minutes. Great sincerity but endless repetition of the theme: "Trust Jesus and he will look after you." I agree thoroughly, but after forty minutes doubts were beginning to slip in. Was the parish priest protesting too much? Did he himself have secret doubts? Was he worried that Gerhard Maria Wagner should never have been ordained?[6]

To get myself into shape for the first semester and the papal conclave, I am going off to Frascati for lunch on Saturday— with three Irish students.

Love to all and keep battling on with life. You are GREAT. But I still would love to see you settled into Glynneath [her house in Frankston, outside Melbourne]. Do I need a security picture, "Maev is in Glynneath, and all's well with the world"? Con amore, Gerald.

Gregorian University, Rome, November 12, 1978.

[This letter refers to my nephews, Stewart and James Peters, to an Italian friend Mimi Sbisà, and to Bishop Kennedy, an auxiliary of the Archdiocese of Adelaide, South Australia.]

My dear Maev,

I am just waiting for a call from Stewart, who is flying in from Tel Aviv. Then we have to decide who does the heroic act and meets James at the airport at 5.30 a.m. tomorrow morning. [Stewart did.]

Bishop Phil Kennedy carried home that letter you received from me. In fact, Phil flew out the very hour Pope John Paul

---

6   On January 31, 2009, Pope Benedict XVI appointed Wagner an auxiliary bishop of Linz, Austria. But two weeks later Wagner himself requested that the appointment be withdrawn. It had already generated strong opposition, prompted by his extreme views (e.g. that the Harry Potter novels revealed Satanism and that the sins of the people of New Orleans had caused hurricane Katrina).

died. By the way, Count Leo Ceschi's godson, Leo Maasburg, is in my first-year class (of 160). An added incentive to get myself up to Vicenza [where Ceschi lived] one day.

The editors of that Italian monthly *Ad Gentes* [on missionary activity] have translated your article into Italian, like it *very* much, and are ravenous for a little more. They want to make it a star feature. Could you face doing about seven to eight typed pages on the Church (or rather the Churches), their arrival in the country, the way the people received the message, and the place of the Churches in the development of the country? (I take it the magazine would like more emphasis on the Roman Catholic Church, but would not want the other Churches to be ignored.) And then three to four pages on the style of life, the culture, art, social order, economic character and structure of Papua New Guinea? That sounds as if you would need to write hundreds of pages! However, they only want three to four pages on that. I hope this won't be a bother to you. But Assunta Ozzi and the others liked your article greatly and want to expand it with the additions indicated. There is no great rush, incidentally.

I hope those wretched people on the appointments committee at Melbourne University realize the error of their ways, and rethink matters to the point of inviting you. How foolish can people be! [Equipped with a doctorate from Columbia University, New York, with teaching experience at Hunter College, New York and with some years heading a department at the University of Papua New Guinea, Maev had applied to become head of social studies at Melbourne University. The committee, chaired by Eric D'Arcy, later the Archbishop of Hobart (Tasmania), turned her down: "a strong candidate but has not yet headed a department at a major university."

This "Catch 22" reasoning would mean that no one could ever become head of such a department!]

Dimension Books is much better at mailing books when I ask them to do so. *A Month with Jesus* arrived promptly out in Australia. Paulist Press who have published *The Second Journey* are rather remiss about such matters. Hence no copies have yet hit Australia for the family or for the shops.

I gave Mimi Sbisà a call, and she seemed enthusiastic about Stewart and me (plus James, I suppose) coming up to Castel Gandolfo next week.

Does Moira have Genevieve Albers' address in Seattle? I hope I am spelling her name right. When I saw her in Seattle last year, she spoke about coming to Rome. With a new pope, I might encourage her to do so. She just might think that the Gregorian was worth putting some money into, instead of giving it all to Seattle University. The Greg still staggers along in the red. I used to think the Vatican might terminate my stay here. But it might be the bailiffs. Anyway, if you can dig her address out of Moira's book, I would be glad to have it—for the aforesaid intention. [Albers, a friend of my sister Moira, was heir to the Carnation Company, acquired in 1984 by Nestlé.] Much love, Gerald.

Gregorian University, Rome, May 8, 1979.

[This letter refers to Bill Daniel, a moral theologian and fellow Australian Jesuit.]

My dear Dympna, Thank you very much for your letter. I am glad you smell only roses and nothing of the canal's "Friday afternoon stench" [she lived near the Elsternwick Canal,

Melbourne]. I would love to see Ian Guthridge and wife (Bettina?), Peter Game etc. [friends of Dympna, who were to visit Rome]. I am sandwiching this letter in between two classes and a meeting with the dean. Someone is flying back to Australia tomorrow, and will take the letter.

I leave Rome on July 5 and via the United States reach Melbourne on July 17 at 12.30 on Pan Am 811. Via Fr Bill Daniel, I have booked myself at the Jesuit Theological College in Parkville. If you are free to meet me [at the airport], that would be lovely. Plans are to stay in Melbourne July 17–23, and then after a bit of work in Adelaide to return to Melbourne August 4–25. Moira may have a party in mind, August 6 or so. By the way, could you let Moira know that the Pope will be out of Rome June 2–10, which means her friends (the Franks) will miss him here.

Please excuse this miserable little letter, but Rome continues to be inordinately busy. Much love, Gerald.

Gregorian University, Rome, June 3, 1979.

My dear Moira and Jim, Welcome to Paris! Thanks for the May 15th letter. I fly direct from Rome to New York on July 5. No stop in Ireland, alas. I hope to be there in 1980.

August 15 would be fine for a little party. I can leave a few names in Melbourne, after I arrive on July 17. Let's see about my staying [at her farm in Kilmore] when I return to Melbourne from Adelaide. That would be lovely.

At the moment I am sorting out the program for lectures in Melbourne. Had dinner on Friday with the Whitlams [Gough Whitlam former Australian prime minister and his wife Margaret] and Don Dunstan [former premier of South Australia]. Much love, Gerald. [I recall nothing from the dinner conversation, except that Margaret Whitlam urged me to complete my sentences.]

Jesuit Theological College, Parkville, August 22, 1979.

[This letter refers to Nicholas and Dympna Mary, two of my sister Dympna's children.]

My dear Dympna, Thanks for the great hospitality during my rushed stay in Melbourne. The "Chinese" evening was a lovely ending to it all.

Please give my love to Dympna Mary, and tell her I was sorry not to see her at the end, as well as at the beginning of my stay. I was delighted that your studies are going so well. I am sure that—among other things—you have done a lot for Nicholas and Dympna Mary by your success at Churchill [the Gippsland campus of Federation University] and Monash University. [Nicholas was eventually to take a PhD at the University of Cambridge.]

At the moment I feel like taking a great, big breath and hope that India is not going to prove too tiring. Thanks again, Dymps. Much love, Gerald.

St Joseph's Seminary, Mangalore, September 8, 1979.

My dear Dympna, Tonight I take the Malabar Express down to Cochin for the next leg of my Indian visit. They have kept me busy enough here: four lectures on Christology to the ninety theologians at St Joseph's Seminary, an informal seminar (on movements in the Church) with the staff, two afternoon sessions for sisters (250 the first day and 200 the second—was I losing my audience?), a morning lecture to college students (where I definitely lost my audience), an afternoon with 45 diocesan priests, morning Masses at several convents (including a cloistered monastery and a convent of Apostolic Carmel), and a Mass for the Bethany Sisters, a local congregation of well over a thousand sisters who have a novitiate–high school–business school compound about ten miles out of town.

The Indians can really lay on a warm welcome. At the convent of the Bethany Sisters, three novices wearing sarees danced a welcome, and the superior said they felt they were receiving Jesus, as Martha and Mary did long ago in the original Bethany. I said I felt like Lazarus coming back to his sisters from the dead.

The permanent chaplain out there turned out to be an ex-naval commander who knew Cardinal James Knox [former Archbishop of Melbourne] and studied for the priesthood at the Beda College in Rome. We shared a bungalow for the night, or rather I shared his bungalow. His presence was reassuring as the area is infested with vipers and other snakes. But the sisters assured me that their founder had given his blessing years ago, and none of them have ever been bitten.

Yesterday I visited a couple of Jain temples: the temple of 1000 pillars in Moodbidri and one on top of a huge rock near Karkal ("black rock"). From there, a 35-foot high statue of a pleasant looking god called "Armstrong" views the countryside. The supreme deity, Brahma, represented by a small statue, keeps an eye on Armstrong (who, incidentally, was carved from a single piece of stone and put in position during the 14th century). Much love to all, Gerald. [On November 17, 1979, the London *Tablet* published my article, "Letter from India."]

Gregorian University, Rome, October 4, 1979.

My dear Dympna, This is just a hasty note to find out if the Sicily trip is still on. I would love to be there with you over Christmas (December 22–29). But, if not, there is a job I need to do in Oxford: fixing up the papers of an Australian Jesuit who died [James Lyons]. This can always be put off until later in 1980. But if I were free over Christmas, I would slip over to England and despatch the job then.

I have really been wondering what has been happening in Papua New Guinea and how that affects Maev's movements. Since leaving Sydney for India on August 31, I have no news about the Rooney case etc. [I referred to the murder on Manus Island of Wes Rooney, the husband of the politician Nahau Rooney. Both were friends of Maev.] So I would be glad to hear what plans/news are.

I hope you got my letter from India. A mountain of things to attack here as term starts. Much love, Gerald.

Gregorian University, Rome, February 23, 1980.

[This letter refers to Margaret Manion, Professor of Fine Arts at the University of Melbourne 1979–95, the first woman to be appointed to an established chair at that university.]

My dear Moira, I am taking advantage of Margaret Manion's kindness to get this letter to you. She has just finished work in various museums etc., and is flying home tomorrow, to face the new term at Melbourne University.

Yes, Gammarellis [a famous ecclesiastical tailor in Rome] still had Uncle Jim's measurements. The chap there was delighted about the business, as Uncle's last (of many) items bought from them was in 1965 [the fourth and final session of the Second Vatican Council]. The soutane with red piping etc. is being made. It will come to 194,000 lire, and should be ready in a few weeks. I will either airmail it, or else give it to someone to carry out to Australia. I will order the papal blessings and send them out with the cassock. [In May 1980, Bishop O'Collins was to celebrate fifty years as a bishop, and Moira gave him a new soutane or cassock for the occasion.]

A very happy birthday on March 23. Sorry to cut this short, but we are just starting the second semester and that fills up the day relentlessly. My love to you all, Gerald. PS. Please tell James [her son] that I will have him rowing on the Tiber when he returns. [Alas, I never managed to launch him on the Tiber.]

Washington, DC, April 4, 1983.

Dear Dympna, Thanks very much for the letter. The wedding [of our niece Marion Peters to Rick Brown] was a great success, and I found Rick's parents and sister most agreeable and intelligent people. On April 7, I head back to Rome for the rest of our second semester.

From late June till late July, I will be lecturing in the States, mainly in the New York area. Then I expect to be able to spend August in Melbourne—based at the Jesuit Theological College in Parkville.

Being here in Washington for the wedding has given me the chance of seeing one or two theological colleagues at

Georgetown University and elsewhere. Everywhere there are flowers in Washington, with the cherry trees especially beautiful. All very different from Rome, where we have to be content with azaleas and later with roses.

Peace and love to you all, Gerald. PS. Thanks very much for the birthday gift.

University of San Francisco, July 15, 1984.

[This letter refers to a nephew, Justin Peters, his sister Joanna, and her husband Bob.]

My dear Dympna, A very happy birthday on July 31. I will be celebrating it here at the University of San Francisco. On 3 August I finish my summer course (35 students on Christ's resurrection) and leave for New York, Rome, and Jerusalem. [At a meeting of Jesuit deans of theology (who included Jon Sobrino from El Salvador), held in Tantur, outside Jerusalem, I represented the dean of theology at the Gregorian.] I talked to Joanna on the phone the other day, heard Douglas having a little cry in the background, and look forward to being allowed to push him down Fifth Avenue. Thanks for *Year One*, which I look forward to reading when I get back to Rome at the very beginning of September.

Tomorrow the Democratic Convention starts right on our doorstep. Then before the end of the month, the Olympic Games in Los Angeles. California seems busier than ever. I am hoping to meet a young Italian friend, Giuseppe Lamaro, whose brother is yachting for Italy in the Games. Giuseppe, an airline pilot, wants to arrive a few days ahead of time, so that he can visit San Francisco etc. Two very old relatives of his (aged 94 and 85) live just a short distance from our campus.

I couldn't see Justin who was about to move to Miami when I arrived in this country. But we talked on the phone. Between Rome and San Francisco, I had a very relaxing weekend in New York with Joanna and Bob. That excellent novel *The Name of the Rose* by Umberto Eco provided just the right reading between Rome and Washington, with the last chapters to read between Washington and San Francisco. It has, among other things, put me into the mood for the days in Umbria at the end of August. [That was my first visit to Umbrian friends, Marcello and Vincenzina Mongardo, who lived in Foligno but also had a house in Trevi, surrounded by olive groves. Umbria was home to such mystics as St Francis of Assisi, St Clare, and St Angela of Foligno.] Warmest best wishes to all the family. Much love, Gerald.

Gregorian University, Rome, January 2, 1985.

My dear Moira, Thanks very much for your letter and the cutting from *The Herald* [Melbourne daily paper]. It was good of Archbishop Frank Little to be so generous in his remarks [about a book of mine].

On December 31, I went to the Church of the Gesù to celebrate the end of the year, see 1985 in, and also update my photographs with the Pope. He comes to that church every New Year's Eve, and afterwards meets the community (of which I am also a member). Belonging to two houses means more work, but it also has such benefits.

You asked about my dates. Over Easter (April 3–13) I will be in England, then back here at the Gregorian till June 15 or at the very latest June 16. Then I fly to the East coast of the States, give some lectures in Providence, Rhode Island, pass through New York, lecture at the University of Notre Dame, stop briefly in San Francisco, and arrive in Australia around July 19. I will be in Melbourne until the end of August, and then back to Rome. So we can certainly catch up in Australia, and maybe also in Rome.

Thanks very much for contributing to the Pembroke Scholar Fund. It you like to, it could be good to contribute something directly (in my name) to Pembroke College, Cambridge— mentioning perhaps that you have also contributed to the Pembroke Scholar Fund in Australia. Address: Valence Mary Endowment Fund, Pembroke College, Cambridge CB2 1RF, England. The College was very good to me, but, more importantly, a contribution keeps my name alive there for the next decade or two, in case any of the family or others could be helped by me to be accepted by Pembroke. Much love, Gerald.

Gregorian University, Rome, February 23, 1986.

My dear Moira, Tomorrow a friend is returning to Melbourne and will take this letter with him. A very happy birthday on March 23 and a great wedding anniversary on April 6. Please wish Frank O'Collins [a nephew] the best from me on his twenty-first. It should be March 14.

At present [as dean of the theology faculty] I have almost finished putting together our theology program for 1986/87. That has kept me off the streets, except for Mass last Friday evening in the rooms where St Ignatius lived and worked during his last years. The Mass involved the eight doctoral students I have in Rome. Afterwards we had a drink and a pizza together. They always enjoy these occasions very much. It makes the loneliness of the long-distance researcher more bearable. They share with one another what they are doing and how far they are along. On Tuesday last I had my first kosher meal in Rome. Two professors from the Hebrew University (Jerusalem) visited the Gregorian and signed an agreement of friendship and collaboration between the two universities. The document was drawn up in Hebrew and Latin. Afterwards several of us joined the couple (they are husband and wife) for a meal in Trastevere. Oddly enough there are no kosher *trattorie* in the Jewish ghetto. I was glad the kosher regulations don't cover wine, as the kosher effect on food is to produce a second-rate Italian lunch.

When your birthday comes around, it always makes me think how incredibly lucky I have been having you as a sister. You have been a wonderful friend and support all my life. I always remember you with much love and gratitude.

Did I tell you my summer plans? I stay in Rome till around July 6 and then go to England—partly for a holiday and partly to give a short retreat to priests in Sheffield and a three-day Christology institute in London. On August 2, I am off to South America, a flag-showing operation in Brazil, Argentina, Chile, and Colombia. I need to know more about that continent if I am to help the Latin Americans who come to study at the Gregorian. Virtue may be rewarded, and I hope to make contact with some possible visiting or even permanent professors for our theology faculty. I get back to Rome at the very beginning of September.

The enclosed flyer reports the launching of two books written by professors of the Gregorian. They come off the tongue so well—those names like Rino Fisichella and Carlo Rochetta. Much love to Jim [Moira's husband] and the whole family, Gerald. PS Please tell Justin [her son] that Boris, his plant, is thriving and much admired. [Justin had been visiting Rome and left a plant for my office.]

Gregorian University, Rome, March 7, 1986.

To whom it may concern at the Australian consulate in Rome, 1) As you see, I can produce all the documentation needed to renew my passport, including the 1976 passport renewed at your office. My 1981 passport was also renewed at the Australian consulate in Rome.

2) I can produce an "Extract of Entry" for my birth in St Kilda, Victoria (June 2, 1931) from March 12, 1984, but it does not show the names of my parents.

3) Do you really want me to go through the motions of ordering from Australia a certificate showing the names of my parents? You can check the latest Australian *Who's Who* (in your library) which gives my parents' names. You can check my biography of my grandfather, *Patrick McMahon Glynn* (Melbourne University Press and Cambridge University Press, 1965) which gives my parents' names (copy provided). You can check other books I have published which establish that I was born in Australia (copies provided).

In 1986 I presided at the Anzac Day service in Rome, and am thoroughly well known to various Australian diplomats like Sir Peter Lawler. You will find my name on file with the Australian embassy in Rome since 1974. To put it mildly, I am not exactly unknown as an Australian citizen either in Rome or back in Melbourne.

If you insist, I will request from Australia a birth certificate giving my parents' names. But I do so under protest. I will register my protest with members of the Australian Parliament, starting with a senator [John Langmore] who will be visiting me before Easter. Yours faithfully, Gerald O'Collins, s.j.

Gregorian University, Rome, March 8, 1986.

My dear Moira, Once again a very happy birthday on March 23. Could I bother you for a little favour? To renew my passport I need an original, full birth certificate showing names of both parents from the Government Statistician, 295 Queen Street, Melbourne, Vic. 3000; tel. 609 9900. The fee is $18.

I found it amazing that, even though I have held a passport since 1964 and renewed it twice at the Australian embassy in Rome itself (1976 and 1981), I now need an original, full birth certificate. If that is the law, the law is an ass. Or else the consular officials in Rome are wooden in their application of the law.

I enclose a copy of the letter I wrote to our consulate. I will send the same to John Langmore and one or two others in parliament. It seemed amazing that last year I presided at the Anzac Day service here and this year I have to prove my Australian citizenship.

As you see, I feel strongly about this. Maybe I should take Mother's famous clinical view of things. Thanks a million and much love, Gerald. PS I was born in St Kilda and the official number of the entry is 15081.

Gregorian University, Rome, January 2, 1987.

My dear Moira, Thanks very much for your Christmas present which helped to raise the consumption of "spumante." Official sources claim that over the holiday period we Italians despatched twenty million bottles of the stuff.

I hope the wedding [of her daughter Bronwen] went off well. Do you feel a sense of relief now? With all three girls married, you can enjoy, more as a "spectator", the weddings to come? Monica Ellison [a London cousin] was happy to have all the news from Australia. She was proudly showing off Samuel, her first grandchild (by Juliet). Emma is getting married on June 6 to a Frenchman, who works in air-traffic control in Paris. He is a delightful guy, as is, I believe, Juliet's husband, Jean. Monica's oldest, Jane, leaves in a few days to work in the BBC office in New York, where she will produce "Panorama" and, I think, another program.

Yesterday I went out at midday to see Spartaco (a white-haired gentleman of about sixty) and a younger associate dive into the Tiber at midday from the Ponte Cavour. Hundreds of people were there, as usual, to see this tribal ceremony. Down on the river, lots of boats were gathered for the annual New Year's Day regatta. After that diversion I ducked inside to watch the Strauss concert from Vienna. Von Karajan (who is not much longer for this world) conducted in a wonderful kind of challenge to death. Visually the show is extraordinarily beautiful (the ballet dancers, the horses from the Vienna riding school, the flowers given every year by the people of San Remo etc). In the middle of all these images of beauty, there was von Karajan keeping the music going till he dies.

Please wish Stewart a very happy birthday on the 3rd. Like all your children he has been a great friend to me. Much love to you and Jim, Gerald.

Gregorian University, Rome, March 9, 1987.

My dear Moira, Thank you for your letter and all the family news. I am so glad the wedding and Christmas were such good times.

A very happy birthday on the 23rd. Every time that date comes around, I think of how much you have done for me—not least in showing me what a great human and Christian life can be. Have a happy celebration that day. I will be spending it, or at least the afternoon, running a seminar on the 1985 Synod of Bishops in Rome, slipping into a meeting of rectors of various colleges who have students at the Gregorian, and then catching the tail end of a doctoral defence. The candidate is from Manila, and arranged the date so that his bishop, none other than Cardinal Sin, can attend.

Next Sunday, Jürgen Moltmann arrives from Tübingen to give a month-long course (on eschatology or death and the other "last things") at the Gregorian. He always recalls with pleasure the visit to your home in early 1973 (at the time of the Eucharistic Congress in Melbourne). He is still exceptionally energetic. I am trying to stop him taking on too many extras when he's here in Rome.

Dates? I leave Rome on June 22, and via New York (a few days), the University of Notre Dame (two weeks of teaching), and the University of San Francisco (two weeks of teaching), I reach Sydney around July 27. I will be in Melbourne by August 1, to stay for three weeks before heading home to Rome via Perth.

Spring is showing through here. With women's day yesterday, the whole city seems to be covered with wattle blossom—"mimosa" they call it. Much love to you all, Gerald.

Gregorian University, Rome, February 29, 1988.

My dear Moira, Thanks for your letter and a very happy birthday on March 23. I was delighted to learn that you and Jim will have another grandchild shortly.

In case I forget, my summer looks like this: leave Rome around June 17, do some lectures in the USA (Burlington, Vermont, and Dallas); visit St Louis and New York; go to Bogotà around July 8; then around July 23 a week in London; the month of August in Nuremberg (with the Jesuits at the Caritas Pirckheimer House), and back to Rome on August 31.

Work here [as dean of theology] remains fascinatingly international and intercultural. The first day back after the New Year brought me an Italian bishop (from the Marches near Loreto), a lady from Viterbo, an African, and a Colombian girl studying in Louvain. That was a quiet morning. These days fifteen or twenty students normally come by each morning with a great variety of needs and requests.

This year I have started going to concerts once or twice a month on Tuesday evenings. Often there is an Italian judge (Zucconi) next to me, a cousin of a colleague here at the Gregorian University. Currently he is presiding over the appeal of a number of Sicilian *Mafiosi* who last year received massive sentences. During the day Zocconi is surrounded by the police. But he comes alone at night to the concerts. Maybe *Mafiosi* hitmen operate only by day? At any rate I accompany Zocconi only halfway home when the concerts end, excuse myself, and take the *via dei Coronari* back to the Gregorian. A courageous man, Zocconi could have refused to preside over the appeal.

Much love to you all, Gerald.

PS Please tell young Jim [her son] that the girls at Gucci's were asking after him.

Gregorian University, Rome, March 20, 1988.

My dear Moira, Sorry to bother you with this request, when you are getting ready to head off to the USA. But maybe it will take only a moment to verify Granny's name and date of birth and then the details about her children. I lost my copy of the family tree, and need it, as someone can fix up the charts right now for the book I may publish one day [*A Midlife Journey* (Ballarat/Leominster: Connor Court/Gracewing, 2012)]. This year I have had an assistant, an American who is a wizard. Before he returns to his post in the USA, he will do a fine family tree for me.

As you can see, there is a lot missing: the family name of Frieda [Uncle Joe's wife] is uncertain, Aunt Madge (was she Margaret?) etc. Thanks a lot. Have a great visit to the States. I will be there in June/July. Happy birthday tomorrow. Much love, Gerald.

Pereira, Colombia, August 17, 1988.

[This letter refers to Moira's daughter Joanna, her husband Bob, their two children, Douglas and Adelaide, and to the Browns, parents-in-law of Moira's eldest daughter, Marion.]

My dear Moira, I am writing this letter in Pereira (Colombia), but will probably mail it next week when I arrive in London. Much of the week in New York I spent correcting proofs and doing an index for a book (my fourth on Jesus' resurrection) and visiting Joanna, Bob, Douglas, and Adelaide. I was allowed to nurse and feed Adelaide, but not yet give her a bath and change her diapers. Jo was just back from hospital after her gall-bladder operation, hobbling a bit but visibly getting stronger every day. Adelaide is as pretty a six-week-old baby as I have ever seen.

As it happened, I lunched with Dr Eugene McCarthy, a professor at New York Hospital, who spoke highly of Jo's surgeon. Gene and his wife Maureen have endowed a chair in theology at the Gregorian—in memory of their eldest son who died in an accident a few years ago. Before lunch Maureen took me for a drink in the patrons' lounge at the Metropolitan Museum. She wanted me to meet a young woman doctor whom she and Gene have helped through various traumas and who is getting married very soon to a West Australian in Perth. I looked across the sumptuous lounge at two portraits: "Romney and Reynolds?," I asked. The works in question turned out to be by Romney and Raeburn. But I felt satisfied with getting 50% right.

The night of July 3/4 I spent with Beau and Shirley Brown over in Westfield, New Jersey. They had several charming friends to supper. When asked what I have been writing and publishing lately, I spoke vaguely of books on the Bible. How could you tell a totally Jewish party that you have recently put out a book on Jesus' resurrection and have another one coming shortly on the same topic? Maybe I should be totally frank with the Browns and their close friends.

Incidentally, when wandering around New York I had pressed into my hand a leaflet advertising Jews for Jesus Travel Agency. I don't know what they are like as travel agents. On the theological level, the leaflet said nothing about the Church and the sacraments. But it had a pretty high doctrine on Jesus coming from heaven, dying, and rising from the dead to be the Saviour of the human race.

The terrible extremes of wealth and poor misery in New York struck me once again. On the bus coming in from La Guardia airport I spotted two brilliantly coloured pheasants scuttling into the long grass at the side of the freeway.

The hospitality in Colombia was overwhelming. Much love, Gerald.

Gregorian University, Rome, October 22, 1988.

[This letter refers to my niece Marion, her husband Rick, their daughter Abigail, my brother Glynn, and my brother-in-law Jim, as well as to my being dean of theology at the Gregorian.]

My dear Moira, Abigail looks a treat. Aimee [Rick's sister] brought me a photo of Abigail at 48 hours of age. You and Jim must be thrilled. I am looking forward greatly to seeing her, Marion, and Rick next July.

Glynn phoned yesterday and even cracked a joke—no mean

feat at that distance and a good sign of recovery [from cancer] as well.

Tomorrow the Pope has a Mass in St Peter's for the opening of the academic year. It gives me a chance of updating my photos with him. Deans *et hoc genus omne* [and all this kind of person] can concelebrate the Mass and so get to shake his hand afterwards in the sacristy.

Mornings I spend locked into my office, as students still come by to be enrolled, to check courses etc. What little time remains I am trying to write two articles for the *Anchor Bible Dictionary*: on "crucifixion" (5,000 words) and "salvation" (15,000 words). The piece on salvation is a hopeless task, as the whole Bible directly or indirectly concerns salvation. At any rate, it was good to be asked...[the rest of the letter is missing].

Gregorian University, Rome, September 3, 1989.

My dear Moira and Jim, Thanks for that great party on August 8 and the excellent weekend at the farm. Bylands [the locale of their property near Kilmore, Victoria] is beautiful, even if the kangaroos sometimes refuse to show themselves.

On the flight back, at least for the sector Singapore/Rome, there was a local bishop from Papua New Guinea, born near Rabaul but with a diocese not that far from Port Moresby. He must be the only leader I have ever met from PNG who does not know Maev [my sister]. The exception that proves the rule? Apropos of bishops, from Sydney to Singapore there was an Anglican bishop from Mozambique who had been invited to the recent synod in Sydney on women's ordination.

With so many being killed and maimed in his country, he has other things on his mind, and was hurrying home because he had learned that there might be a break-through in peace negotiations.

The more than sixty bishops from the USA, plus Frank Little [Archbishop of Melbourne], arrived a week ago for their course, which seems to be going along happily. On Friday last, I offered one lecture on St Peter and another on St Mary Magdalene. Next Thursday I speak to them again, in the meantime dropping around for meals at the Casa Santa Maria where they are all staying. You remember the Casa? It's the college next door to us, where Dennis Sheehan, that engaging priest from Boston, lived for a good number of years.

It was a great joy seeing you both again, catching up with Sheila [a sister-in-law of Moira] and having the chance of seeing the children and grandchildren. I enjoyed them immensely—right to that last evening and supper with young Jim [Moira's son]. Much love, Gerald.

Gregorian University, Rome, January 1, 1990.

Dear Moira, Here we go into the nineties. 1989 had its bright moments and some shadows. Back in April, a lecture by Seamus Heaney on W. B. Yeats (occasioned by the 50th anniversary of Yeats's death) restored my faith in the English language. A guest that evening at the Irish College, Heaney combined wonderful words, wit, kindness, and precise criticism in a masterly way. A month or two later he was elected the new professor of poetry at Oxford University.

Mid-June took me out to the Vatican Observatory in Castel

Gandolfo for a weekend meeting with astronomers and philosophers. We didn't solve the problems of the universe but it was an intellectual feast, not to mention the final supper in the gardens of the papal villa.

In July I lectured at the University of Notre Dame and the University of San Francisco, and then in the Christchurch diocese (my first visit to New Zealand since 1975). Each morning during that week in New Zealand, I looked across the Canterbury plains to the snow-covered Alps which seemed fresh and near in the winter sunshine. After a holiday in Australia, I was back in Rome at the end of August to lecture to sixty US bishops taking a three-week long updating course at the Gregorian University. Term began in October with the presentation of a book on John Henry Newman. The following day, October 20, we visited the Italian President in the Quirinal Palace to give him a copy of the book, *Luce nella Solitudine* [Light in the Solitude]. Cossiga knows his Newman well, and is an honorary fellow of Oriel, Newman's old college in Oxford.

In November I was down on a flying visit to lecture at a teachers training college in Messina. Returning to Rome, I found myself surrounded on the bus and plane by the Clan rugby club from Messina, off to play a game against a team from Lazio. Wonderful rowdies, they pretended to be as tough as nails but were real softies—like their counterparts who play rugby in Australia and England.

Does work for TV count among the bright moments? At all events, I said my thing ("Italy brings out the best in you") for an hour-long film on Australians who live and work in Italy. Around the same time (last April), I did an interview for an

Irish TV film, a retrospective on the Second Vatican Council.

An early shadow in the year was the death last April of Enrico Massa. An Italian lawyer, who had his office just off the Via Veneto, he was a loyal and amusing friend for years. Then in November we all mourned the martyrdom of the six Jesuits in El Salvador. I have never seen the Church of the Gesù so packed as it was for the Mass on November 16. Their death cut through the trivia to the real point of our lives. Older Jesuits grieved, while the younger ones seemed also grateful and proud.

Thank you very much for your Christmas gift. We had a superb, warm Christmas season here. Students resume on January 8. In the meantime I am trying to catch up on a thousand items. Peace and love to you all, Gerald.

Gregorian University, Rome, November 6, 1990.

My dear Moira and Jim, October has come and gone. It was a good month. On the 13th a mega-Mass in St Mary Major's launched simultaneously a) the Ignatian Year in Rome—1990/91 being both 500 years since St Ignatius was born and 450 years since the Society of Jesus was officially approved—and b) the academic year for the Gregorian Consortium [a name for the Gregorian University, the Biblical Institute, and the Oriental Institute combined]. The big crowd was welcomed by a Welsh monsignor, once a manufacturer of ladies underwear and now the apostolic administrator of the basilica. You remember the fabulous mosaics in that fifth-century building? Even perhaps the band of animals high above the altar? I saw those little beasts begin to scuttle off into the corners when they heard some hunting horns. The

"Rallye du Parc aux Cerfs" came from Versailles, put on their scarlet uniforms, and blew their brass at four points during the ceremony. Later in the evening they were at it again—in the Piazza Navona.

On October 20, I went out to Fiumicino to pick up a Lutheran bishop and his wife and bring them to a pensione run by Brigittines just off the Piazza Farnese. We hardly got in the door before Bishop Lohse met and hugged an old (Catholic) friend, Bishop Brandenburg (from Stockholm) who happened to be staying in the same pensione. Another first for me! Never before have I seen two German bishops hugging each other. The times they are a changing, not just ecumenically. A fine biblical scholar, Bishop Lohse is lecturing at the Gregorian for six weeks on Paul's Letter to the Romans. [During World War II, Lohse and Brandenburg served together in the German navy.]

On October 23, I blessed the wedding of two young friends in St Agnes, Piazza Navona. The church and adjacent buildings may be taken over by Opus Dei money. But the Dorias, to whom the whole complex belongs, are fighting back. The case will be heard next month. Three of the four witnesses (at the wedding, not for the case) were women. More trustworthy than male witnesses? (See the women in the Easter chapters of the four Gospels.) With Mary and David hitched, I have gotten through my third wedding for the year, the other two being in Venice (April) and Albano (June).

The month ended with a Halloween party just off the Spanish Steps. George, a journalist, had taped a horror film from the thirties to make the evening spookier. Boris Karloff and Bela Lugosi went at it hard until they were all dynamited, except for the young American couple who slipped back into normal life. One had to swallow a lot in that film—in particular, a splendid modern castle built in Hungarian woods on the site of a First World War battle.

Jim, a very happy birthday retrospectively on the 20th. Moira, if you are doing anything for the University of Melbourne, you might put a Christmas gift in for me. The old university did us all proud. Much love, Gerald.

Gregorian University, Rome, December 1990.

My dear Moira and Jim, My midsummer visit to Prague was a kaleidoscope of impressions that I want to share with you. By mid-August most of the bright young things of Europe and North America seemed to have converged on the city. It was standing room only on the Charles Bridge, which crosses the broad Vltava (Moldau) River to connect the Old Town and the "Little Quarter," dominated by St Vitus' Cathedral and the royal (now the presidential) castle.

You could listen to hard-rock in the Old Town Square or jazz on the Charles Bridge. Hawkers signalled a return to a market economy, and were selling a broad range of products, from traditional glassware to Red Army caps. "A Midsummer's Night Dream," billed as an "erotic fantasy," was running from July into September. In late August the Rolling Stones came to town for a noisy success. Earlier the same week the first casino had opened.

Under the hot sun, a general euphoria and tanned bodies made it hard to imagine the baton charges, police dogs, and water-cannon sweeps that occurred the previous November, before the nation finally straightened its back and swept away the Communist Party.

On a corner of Narodni Street, where the students were beaten during "the velvet revolution," a theaterette offered hourly video presentations in English and German about those ten days and the events leading up to them. The film included some remarkable shots. A Communist Party official explained to a large crowd of factory workers that the demonstrators in Wenceslaus Square were just a pack of adolescents. "We are not children," chanted the workers. "Resign! Resign!" There were scenes of police, covered by helicopters, driving away visitors who had come to place flowers on the country grave of Jan Palach. As you remember, in 1969 that student had burned himself to death in protest in Wenceslaus Square.

Opposite the French Embassy, graffiti covered a large wall honouring John Lennon. In a dozen languages you were told to support truth, justice, love, and freedom An elegantly written sentence caught my eye: "Peace in the world or the world in pieces." "Students were arrested for writing on this wall," an old friend told me. "The government had those graffiti cleaned off each day. But people kept coming back to write more."

Yet one did not really need the films or the graffiti to remember what the Czechs went through under the Nazis and the Communists. Smart streets have sunk into dust and decay. Many old churches urgently need restoration. Libraries and archives are in a miserable condition. The famous "art nouveau" buildings have lost their brilliance. The whole country is desperate for foreign exchange. You needed no persuasion when told: "The Communists left this country economically and morally bankrupt. Before the Second World War we were among the first ten industrial nations of the world. Now we are forty-seventh."

President Havel's plays are being produced around the world. Across Prague, statues and monuments of Kafka, Kepler, Beethoven, Goethe, Mozart, Dvořák, Emperor Charles IV (who founded the cathedral and the university), St Wenceslaus, St John Nepomucene, St Agnes of Bohemia, and others recall a spiritual and cultural heritage, but it has been almost totally submerged by totalitarian ideologies. Czechoslovakian culture has obviously taken a dreadful beating.

In the Old Town Square curious tourists giggled at the ugliest monument any of us are ever likely to see: a plastic car squatting on toad-like legs and celebrating socialist, technological "success" [the Trabant car].

I joined others who had escaped into the Tym Church for a moment's peace and prayer. A baroque organ, once played by Lord Edward Heath (former British Prime Minister), announced the end of a wedding ceremony. A radiant bride and the warmth of family and friends reflected the optimistic message others had already conveyed to me.

Now back in the seminary of which they had been dispossessed for decades, the Catholic theology faculty of Prague was preparing for the coming academic year. Well over a hundred diocesan seminarians will live and study there again.

Despite economic fragility and transitional tensions, Czechoslovakian Christians and their leaders are planning the spiritual renewal of the nation. This is no easy task. A church of silence and suffering must be reshaped to meet the needs of the next generation.

The Czechoslovakian Church will not be alone in its efforts. Groups and individuals are already coming to offer their help.

An old hand from a developing country [my sister Maev who was with me], however, shared some misgivings: "it reminds me just a little of a country experiencing a post-colonial rush of aid. Everyone has a solution. In both Christian and national life, the local people must decide for themselves and work out their destiny."

A university graduate, now retired, spends her senior years maintaining the Church of Our Saviour in its original baroque splendour. A middle-aged couple from San Francisco shared my joy at this ministry which helps to keep that church a place of prayer for hundreds of students.

Dozens of bicycles caught my eye in the cloister of the Church of St James. They belonged to French boys and girls enjoying Franciscan hospitality there. A stooped brother, who for decades had guarded and cherished his monastery, radiated the joy of one who has fought the good fight and seen the tide turn. He took me through the sacristy into the church itself. In the sanctuary a novice-master was leading four young men in the divine office. Faith is alive and growing in Czechoslovakia. Love, Gerald.

Gregorian University, Rome, 16 January 1991.

My dear Moira, Thank you for your Christmas gift and the Australian card. Once again the koala singing to honour the new-born Jesus proved a smash hit in my office [as dean of the theology faculty].

The pre-Christmas phase of first semester slipped by with a few highlights. One was undoubtedly the six-week course on Paul's Letter to the Romans by Eduard Lohse, an excellent exegete and retired (Lutheran) bishop. A truly great Christian, he made his visit here a total success, with never a whimper from the Vatican. In fact, Cardinal Joseph Ratzinger [the future Pope Benedict XVI] came along to Lohse's public lecture (on what Paul thought of Peter's ministry)— positive and honest stuff, straight out of the New Testament.

On November 1, I made my first visit to the generalate of the Dominicans, Santa Sabina, a fifth-century basilica which has belonged to the Dominicans since 1219. The Dominicans gave a lunch to a group of Ambassadors to the Holy See, about fifteen of them who form a prayer group. Now how about that! They became tired of just meeting for social occasions. At the November meeting I offered them some reflections on John 21.

One of my great discoveries of last year was the music of Domenico Zipoli (1688–1726). A student of Alessandro Scarlatti (1660–1725) and organist at the Church of the Gesù here in Rome, he gave up his success to become a Jesuit and work on our "reductions" in South America. Before being ordained, he died of tuberculosis in northern Argentina. The wonderfully cheerful baroque music he composed for/among the Indians was recently discovered. "Beautiful, holy, heroic madness" is what I think when I listen to the tapes.

Just before January 6, I went to record a couple of reflections on the magi for Vatican Radio. My friend there had just been called to the phone and listened for half an hour to an American girl, who was deeply distraught about her boyfriend, a pilot with the forces in Saudi Arabia. Among other things the poor girl wanted a rosary blessed by the Pope [John Paul II] for her friend.

Much love to you, Jim and all the family. Please wish Stewart [her eldest son] a very happy birthday on February 3. Gerald.

Gregorian University, Rome, March 3, 1991.

My dear Moira, A very happy birthday on March 23, and a great wedding anniversary on April 6. I will remember you on both days.

On March 12, the Jesuits assemble in force for a mega-Mass at St Paul's Outside the Walls. It is part of our celebration of the Ignatian year [the year honouring our founder, St Ignatius Loyola]. During Holy Week (March 22–31), I will be out in the hills, making a retreat [a time of silence and prayer] at Villa Cavalletti [Frascati]. After that I am back at the Gregorian till May 17. I will be at the University of San Francisco May 17–27 to receive my honorary doctorate. If I stay a week, it brings down the price of the ticket drastically. It didn't seem right to bill them for the full fare by staying only a few days.

To complete the story, on June 22 I leave for a couple of days in New York, teach at the University of Notre Dame [South Bend, Indiana], see the gang [Moira's daughter Marion, her husband and daughter] in St Louis, and reach Sydney towards the end of July.

Much love to you, Jim, and all the family, Gerald.

Gregorian University, Rome, August 22, 1991.

My dear Moira, Thanks for looking after me so splendidly during my month in Melbourne. I appreciated it all very much: the party in town, the family day on the farm, and all the rest.

Justin [her son], by the way, has a wonderful friend and professional colleague in David Webb [another urologist]. Thanks for making the stay at home a lovely, memorable month. Much love, Gerald.

Gregorian University, Rome, September 16, 1991.

[This letter refers to Ed Kirby, a family friend from World War II, when he served in the US Marines.]

My dear Moira, Tomorrow I am off to Pembroke College [Cambridge], and my Irish passport will enjoy its maiden voyage. I picked it up a couple of days ago at the Irish consulate. Thanks very much for all your help with that. I feel thoroughly Australian AND European now.

I had an excellent run home to Rome via Perth and Bangkok. I have hardly ever had a smoother journey. Watch out next time? Or is that Irish superstition?

When I return to Rome in January, I will head off on two quick lecture tours: Malta (February 11–14) and Los Angeles (March 16–20). On the LA visit, I hope to be able to see Ed Kirby at San Diego. In haste but with much love to all, Gerald.

Pembroke College, Cambridge, October 13, 1991.

[This letter refers to a cousin Fr James Dynon, s.j., an aunt Eileen Glynn, my brother-in-law Jim Peters, my brother Jim, his wife Posey, her sister's family [the Spanoghes], and her niece Sarah.]

My dear Moira, Thanks for another example of your unfailing love in sending me a copy of the order of service for Jim

Dynon. It made me even happier to have been with him in late August at Eileen's charming home in Claremont [a suburb of Perth, Western Australia]. I have never in my life visited a retirement village planned to the last shrub and maintained with a meticulous care worthy of English gardeners. Jim sat and chatted in the sun, interested in everyone and full of fun, as ever, despite his 81 years. R.I.P.

Cambridge is full of bicycles, gowns, and vivid faces, as it was in the sixties. Yet I must admit the young look younger these days. The colleges, chapels, winding streets, churches, lawns, gardens, and chimes all fit together like well matured port. The backs are bright with autumn beauty. I had forgotten how beautiful surroundings make you study more intensely, think more quickly, and come up more readily with some fresh ideas. At all events in two weeks I have finished the first chapter for a new book, on the doctrine of Christ [*Christology*: Oxford University Press, 1995].

Last week I ran into two of the tiniest choirboys imaginable, wearing top hats, striped trousers, and minute gowns, and deep in conversation as they swept past me on their way to King's College Chapel.

Last Thursday I gave a sherry party for the freshmen (freshpersons?) on my staircase: a Basque, a German, a Malaysian, three English girls, and two English boys. Several fellows have rooms on the staircase (which ends in a red, neo-gothic tower) but live out of college. An agreeable lot, the young find me an exotic extra.

Jim [Peters], a very happy birthday next Sunday. I shall lift a glass to you over lunch in Cheltenham with Jim, Posey, and the Spanoghes, as we do a post-mortem on Sarah's wedding (the previous day). If you are near a xerox, Moira, maybe you could make a photocopy of this for Stewart/Nola, Justin/Jill, Bronnie/Andy, Mark, James, and Stephen [her six children in Melbourne, along with the spouses of three]. I love them all dearly, but can't write to everyone. From good old Pembroke, with much love, Gerald.

Pembroke College, Cambridge, December 1, 1991.

My dear Moira and Jim, Michaelmas term ends this week, and the captains, kings, and queens depart. Sales will slump at "Fitzbillies," one of the legendary pastry shops of England. Just a few yards along Trumpington Street from Pembroke College, the store is stuffed with cakes, crumpets, Chelsea buns, and what have you. I keep away from there, but may go to the Clare College Chapel next Tuesday for a solemn requiem Mass (in Latin, of course) for the repose of the soul of Mozart. Better late than never?

The fellows of Pembroke are as full of tales as ever. Donald Denman, a retired professor of land economy, was filling me in on the life and hard times of Svetlana. Being Stalin's daughter, after the death (suicide?) of her mother, she became the first lady of the Kremlin before getting through five husbands and coming to take some rooms at Donald's home here in Cambridge for two years. On one occasion her daughter barricaded herself in a downstairs toilet, which mother proceeded to force open. As a memorial to those lively days on Chaucer Road, Donald has left the damaged door as was. The daughter is now married and living in Wales. Svetlana herself is somewhere in the UK, and keeps up sporadic contact with Donald.

A couple of weeks back I saw Beckett's *Waiting for Godot*—no play for a urologist. The play begins with Vladimir, one of the tramps, making it perfectly clear, by word and gesture, that he has a major prostate problem. Now and then the play gets truly serious or even tragic with lines about the swift transition from birth to death: "They give birth astride the grave."

Once again, Moira, you might want to share this letter via xerox with all your family. I love them all dearly but can't write to them individually. Thanks for the Christmas card and have a wonderful visit to the USA. I am leaving Cambridge on January 10, and will be home in Rome on January 22. Much love for Christmas, Gerald.

Pembroke College, Cambridge, December 4, 1991.

[This letter refers to Monica Ellison, a cousin who lived in London with her husband John, and to Janet Harbison, another Irish cousin, who was a brilliant harpist.]

My dear Moira, Last week I went up to Leeds and lectured to the clergy (130 of them) for a couple of days on "Understanding and Preaching Jesus Today." It was out at Hazlewood Castle, once the home of the Vavasour family and now (since 1946) a Carmelite retreat house The chapel dates from the 13th century and displays the skulls of two martyrs, who were hung, drawn, and quartered in York.

John and Monica Ellison may be going out to Australia in a few months time. Now emeritus from the *Express*, John is freelancing as a journalist. Would there be a chance of their visiting the farm?

Janet Harbison, married as you know, lost a baby—a bit traumatic. I hope to see her in Dublin when I go to lecture for Séan Freyne [professor at Trinity College Dublin] around January 16. The Freynes are putting on a party for me—very decent of them, as otherwise it would be hard to catch up with everyone.

Much love to you, Jim, and all the family, Gerald.

Gregorian University, Rome, Easter Sunday 1992.

[This letter refers to my brother Glynn, who came back from a cancer operation to win the 1992 Senior Championship at Metropolitan Golf Club.]

My dear Maev, Happy Easter and welcome back from Vanuatu [a country consisting of a group of islands in the South-West Pacific]. Maybe, however, you prefer Vanuatu to Canberra, especially as winter draws closer?

Glynn is as "bad" or as good as Jack Nicklaus, who as a veteran managed, I think, to have some wins both in the open and the veteran category. On second thoughts, I am not so sure about the open category. At all events he did very well against golfers over twenty years younger. That makes Glynn even greater than Nicklaus. [The year before, aged fifty-seven, in the final of Metropolitan's Men's Club Championship Glynn beat someone who was over thirty years younger.]

On June 12 I head off for the University of San Francisco (three weeks teaching), Dublin, Nuremberg etc., and back to Rome on September 3. In Nuremberg (July 24–August 22), I am c/o Rev. Holzbauer, Caritas Pirckheimer Haus, Königstrasse 64,

8500 Nürnberg 2, Germany. I hope you like the references to Nuremberg in *Believing: Understanding the Creed* [Mahwah, NJ: Paulist Press, 1992; a book written with Mary Venturini].

A glorious spring day here. It makes the suffering and death of thousands over there in ex-Yugoslavia even more terrible. Much love, Gerald.

Gregorian University, Rome, May 14, 1992.

[This letter refers to my brother Glynn and his wife, and to Kate, the sister of my sister-in-law Posey.]

My dear Moira, Thanks very much for your gift and birthday "auguri [best wishes]." Frankly June 2 is the loveliest time of the year to celebrate in Rome—warm without being too hot, and oceans of light right into the evening. But you remember that from being here (for my 50th?).

Glynn and Barbara get back from Florence in a new minutes and are here until Saturday. This evening we are out to dinner with some Italians and Americans, or rather with an Italian family [Lamaro], who have American guests. The Italians have invited the three of us. It is going to be interesting, not only because there is the fourth race of the America's Cup on TV from 8.30, but also because the eldest son of the Italian family will be the commentator on one of the TV channels, presumably the one we will be looking at every now and then. With all the others present either Italians or Americans, we three Australians can take an unprejudiced view of the race. [The American yacht won that race in San Diego, and went on to beat Il Moro di Venezia four to one.]

Gesine Doria is getting married (to a Roman lad) on Sunday May 24—much excitement. She and Massimiliano are taking Don Luigi (an archbishop who worked for years in the household of Pope John XXIII and Pope Paul VI), Don Luca (a curate from Rome who is Massimiliano's friend and my ex-student) and myself out for lunch on Tuesday May 19. It is very thoughtful of the *promessi sposi* to do something like that for the clerical triumvirate; we had already worked out what we are to do in St Agnes. But it will be a good occasion, and will doubtless attract the attention of others in the restaurant. Three clerics and two young things!

On June 12, I leave for the States (address there until July 10: c/o Jesuit Community, University of San Francisco, 650 Parker Avenue, San Francisco, CA 94118). Then via a little teaching in Dublin, I will be at Caritas Pirckheimer Haus, Königstrasse 64, 8500 Nürnberg 2, Germany until August 24. After a quick visit back to England (to teach a mini-course) and catch up with Kate and her gang, I will be home in Rome on September 3. Much love, Gerald.

University of San Francisco, July 1, 1992.

[This letter refers to an old friend from Melbourne, John Batt, a judge of the Supreme Court of Victoria, to Eleanor, a cousin now living in Kerry, to Kate, the sister of my sister-in-law Posey, and to Moira's eldest daughter Marion, wife of Rick and mother of Abigail.]

My dear Moira, Thanks very much for your fax and letter, with all the news. Yes, John Batt was in touch. I miss him, unfortunately, by one day when I visit London.

In Dublin I will be at All Hallows (July 11–17) and after that with Eleanor Harbison for a long weekend. At this point it is probably better to give you my German address (July 24–August 24): Caritas Pirckheimer Haus, Königstrasse 64, 8500 Nürnberg 2, Germany. The last week of August I will be back in England to give some lectures and catch up with Kate and her family, and then home to Rome on September 3. You probably heard that Kate's second daughter, Gigi, is expecting a baby later this year. Her husband, Patrick, like Gigi is a wonderful young person.

You will have a busy Cup time [the racing season culminating with the Melbourne Cup in early November], but it makes me deeply happy that Marion, Rick, and Abbie will be out. I had a meal the other night with Rick's sister and her splendid husband (a clone on your sons). They always make me feel that San Francisco is my home. So does Dan Kendall, a Jesuit on the staff at the University of San Francisco, who did his thesis with me in the 1970s. Much love to you, Jim, and all the family.

Gregorian University, Rome, September 14, 1992.

[This letter refers to the birth of the second daughter of Moira's son Justin, and to Sir James and Lady Gobbo who lived in Melbourne.]

My dear Moira, Thank you very much for your letter, with all the news, especially about the birth of Cecilia Dominique. I had a fax from Jim Gobbo, and will see them in early October. Maybe with Ferruccio Romanin, SJ, who is on a sabbatical from Richmond parish [Melbourne] and arrives in Rome on September 30.

I don't know how to thank you enough for helping me to get my Irish passport. It saves so much time and hassle in

London, Rome, etc. By the time it expires in 2001 (unless I have expired by then), it will have saved me a week of waiting in line, I reckon.

Since returning to Rome on September 3, I have been reading doctoral theses or parts thereof, as well as preparing a lecture for the meeting of the US bishops (in Columbus, Ohio, October 20–21). I will be away from Rome, October 10–22, making a stop in St Louis en route to Columbus. I am also speaking in New Jersey (at Seton Hall University) to some alumni of the Gregorian, and will give Joanna a call [Moira's daughter who lived in New York]. There is no chance of my getting into New York.

Desmond O'Grady [an Australian journalist who lives in Rome] has just made his usual Sunday morning phone call, telling me *inter alia* how the mafia troubles and the Pope's operation kept him busy over the summer.

Please give Jim [her husband] my warmest best wishes on October 20 [his birthday]. Next summer/winter when I am back in Melbourne (through August), what would you both think of a Mass at the farm, gathering all the youngsters one Sunday—in anticipation of the big birthday on October 20 [Jim's eightieth birthday]. I would be very happy to do that, if you would like it. Much love, Gerald.

Gregorian University, Rome, October 1, 1992.

[This letter refers to a nephew Nicholas Coleman.]

My dear Maev, Just a quick note to assure you that I have booked you a single room at Santa Brigida (no curfew, key available, etc.) from December 28 for two weeks. In a fax to

Posey [our sister-in-law] a couple of days ago, I said that I would be doing that. But now the deed is done; the room is ready. Santa Brigida is on the corner of the Piazza Farnese and the street leading to the English College, the via Monserrato. The cost for bed and breakfast is around 90,000 lire. A bit high, but it is a splendid place and the lire has come down a lot against the Australian dollar.[7]

Jim and Shirley Gobbo turn up this weekend, before returning to Australia. They have been in Italy for ten days or more. Talking of Italo-Australians, Fr Ferruccio Romanin has just arrived back, for a two-month stay in Rome. He will brighten us all up.

Next weekend (October 9/10), Nick Coleman, plus wife and son Lachlan, will be overnighting in Rome en route back to Australia On October 10, I am off to the USA to give three lectures, arriving back in Rome on October 22. At the opening of the academic year I wouldn't dream of doing a trip like this. But the key lecture is to the US bishops. So the dean of theology thought I must say yes. Much love, Gerald.

---

7   During her stay in Rome, Maev enjoyed one or two meals with the Prince and Princess Doria Pamphilj. On February 4, 1993, Princess Orietta wrote to Maev: "Dear Maev, A thousand thanks for those beautiful flowers and your sweet note. You really should not have spoilt us. For us it was a great pleasure to see you and hear all your interesting news. Sorry to be so long in writing, but I have only just managed to get your address from Gerry. Life here goes on in the same happy, disorganized way. Our weather has been glorious; so Frank and I have done a lot of wandering around in the late morning sunshine. Hope we will see you back in Rome very soon. Do please remember that we have a guest room which we would love you to occupy if it ever can be of any use to you (so long as we are not away ourselves or someone else in it!). With our love and all good wishes, Frank and Orietta."

Gregorian University, Rome, March 11, 1994.

My dear Moira, A very happy birthday to you on March 23. I hope the family celebrates it well with you. And a very happy wedding anniversary on April 6. Golden minus two! Hooray!

My next book, *Experiencing Jesus*, with a foreword by the Archbishop of Canterbury, bears the date of March 23, 1994. It is one way of celebrating your birthday, even if from a distance. It is a Lent-book for SPCK in London (and probably Paulist Press in New York). It may seem a bit strange, but the British still go in for Lent-books, and SPCK asked me to write one. So why turn down an offer like that? It helped me to go through piles of spiritual notes and throw out 80% as unfit for human/Christian consumption.

During Holy Week (March 26–April 3) I will be out of Rome, not far away at Villa Cavalletti and on retreat. I come back on Easter Sunday itself.

Today a very fine student from Newman College [University of Melbourne], Luke Fraser, turned up. He has just spent a month or more on a scholarship in Moscow, improving his Russian. I introduced him to a visiting professor from Moscow who is lecturing at the Gregorian until March 25. Much love, Gerald.

Gregorian University, Rome, May 1, 1994.

[This letter refers to my brother Glynn and his wife, my niece Joanna, and my niece Marion and her husband.]

My dear Moira, Thank you very much for your letter and generous gift. In a short time I will be heading out for lunch with Glynn and Barbara. They are in fine form, amazingly untouched by jet lag.

Just to make sure you have my dates: I leave Rome on July 1 and via the UK fly into Newark. I expect to spend a few days with Jo and the children. Then lectures, and back to Europe (Germany) on July 20. I return to Rome for a few days on August 24; from August 29 until mid-December, I will be c/o Jesuit Community, Marquette University, Milwaukee, Wisconsin 53233. I expect to spend Thanksgiving with Marion and Rick, but will fly straight back to Europe from Chicago when my sabbatical ends in Marquette.

The azaleas are out in full glory, the swifts back from Africa, and the pilgrims/tourists more cheery than ever.

In my next book, *Experiencing Jesus* (London: SPCK, January 1995), you will pick up two clear references to yourself. I put them in as a personal tribute to a very great sister. Peace and love to all in the family, Gerald.

Gregorian University, Rome, May 29, 1994.

[This letter refers to a number of young Italian friends, to their teacher, Mimi Sbisà and her American husband Lee Shore, and to my brother Jim and his wife Posey.]

My dear Maev, A very happy birthday on June 16, when glasses shall be raised to you on the banks of the Tiber and sundry other places. I had intended to do so after a wedding at Palazzola (the English College villa on Lake Albano), but Luca and Elena have now put their wedding off to a post-July date. You remember my *Friends in Faith* (Mahwah, NJ: Paulist Press, 1989)? He did the chapter on the resurrection and she did the chapter on the church.

They were up there yesterday, with Mimi, Lee, Leonardo, and most of my other young friends—for Mass at 12.30 and then a leisurely picnic in the garden of Palazzola. They brought Pino along in his wheelchair from Velletri. He always asks after you. It's a grace having him here, as well as having small children along. Yesterday there were three of them, playing with the tiny fountain, running up and down the garden, and pulling off their clothes to plunge into the pool.

Friends from different parts of the world have been turning up in Rome to enjoy the long days, the flowers, and the warmth of the sun (not yet violently hot). One came from the Leicester Polytechnic, now renamed De Montfort University. A couple arrived from London and invited me around to their apartment for supper. "But where is it?," I asked. "The Spanish Steps," they told me on the phone from London. "But exactly where?" "Above Keats's house," they said. A marvellous spot to stay, if a bit noisy. You go into Keats's house, head upstairs beyond his apartment, and right on top is a (fairly expensive) apartment for visitors.

I'm off to the USA (via a couple of days in London and Cambridge, to see publishers and Jim/Posey) on July 1, to Nuremberg on July 24, and back to Rome on August 24. Much love, Gerald.

[This letter crossed a fax from Maev, who wrote from Canberra, Australia, on June 1: "A Very Happy Birthday for tomorrow! This is just in case I don't reach you by telephone on the day itself. I am not sure if you have received a card from the wilds of the Highlands of Papua New Guinea. It was a very exciting, only mildly challenging, and thoroughly enjoyable five weeks.

Last night I took the Premier of Manus Province to dinner, along with four other Manusians (I guess that is the right word). He has a Master's from Victoria University in Canada, and is delightful, long-time friend. It was great to catch up, and be able to repay some of his hospitality when I was a researcher in Manus in 1989.

At the moment I have just finished writing an 'expert' opinion on a remote area of the Southern coast of Papua New Guinea, where a port for an oil and gas pipeline is to be developed. At present it can be reached only by boat. If this New Zealand engineering firm wins the contract, I may be all set for another adventure. I shall keep you posted. Much love, dear Gerald."]

Gregorian University, Rome, June 21, 1994.

[This letter refers to my brother Glynn, journalist friend Desmond O'Grady, and Jesuit friend Karl Holzbauer.]

My dear Maev, Today a note arrived from Glynn, saying among other things: "Maev is on the mend, looking well, and should be out of hospital within the week." Please God, you are o.k. You must have spent your birthday [June 16] in hospital. I hope all is well; no one said anything about your being laid up.

We are in the middle of exams here—hundreds of orals to listen to. There may be a shortage of vocations and students of theology elsewhere but not here. It's nice to be wanted. But six days of orals can tax one's academic stamina.

Desmond is not too good. No dramatic discoveries yet, but I can't help feeling that after so many tests they will find something malign in the poor guy. Perhaps I am affected by

Nanni Moretti's latest film, *Caro Diario* [Dear Diary], which relates what doctors put him through for a year. He is a wonderful, 40-year-old Italian actor and director, who wins prizes at Cannes but is simply untranslatable into other languages. He is very Italian. After seeing his *The Mass is Ended*, a kind of Italian version of Bernanos's *Diary of a Country Curate*, I spent an evening with him. "Surely life is not that bad on the outskirts of Rome," I remarked. "It's even worse," Moretti assured me.

I am about to write to Karl Holzbauer to fix up final arrangements for a month in Nuremberg (July 24 to August 24). I leave Rome on July 3, and reach Nuremberg not by the most direct route—via Cambridge and New York. Much love, Gerald.

Marquette University, Milwaukee, September 9, 1994.

[This letter refers to the British writer J. R. R. Tolkien, the saintly American activist Dorothy Day, my niece Marion Peters and her husband, and the great Anglican scholar Henry Chadwick.]

My dear Maev, I hope this catches you before you take off for Papua New Guinea. Late summer is still operative here in Milwaukee, students look cheerful, and I feel liberated (with only a doctoral seminar to run and all the time in the world to read and write lofty theological thoughts).

Marquette has a Tolkien archive, the Dorothy Day archive, and a medieval chapel transported here stone by stone from the French countryside. Joan of Arc prayed in it. It forms the lovely centrepiece of the campus, surrounded by trees, flowers (still happily blooming), and large urns.

I haven't spoken to Marion and Rick yet, but will remedy that over the weekend. I am just back from a guided tour of the University's library, and my head is reeling from all the CD-Roms which allow you to look up anything in the ancient and modern world: e.g., anything the Fathers of the Church ever wrote and any doctoral dissertation ever submitted in the USA.

A good friend of mine and publishing partner, Dan Kendall, SJ, arrives this weekend, en route back from the University of Notre Dame to his domicile at the University of San Francisco. In early October, Henry Chadwick visits from Oxford, to deliver the keynote address at a farewell to George Tavard, a distinguished French theologian who has been at Marquette for a number of years now.

Right next door to the Jesuit Residence at Marquette is the students' theatre, where movies are shown at least once a week. I caught *Schindler's List* last Saturday night. Ben Kingsley as a Jewish accountant practically ran away with the film, I thought.

I hope the doctors have got you absolutely A.1 by this time, and you can resume normal life. Much love, Gerald.

Marquette University, Milwaukee, October 12, 1994.

My dear Moira, Thank you for your card from Sydney. Perfect fall weather here. I head out next Sunday for another walk in the woods to enjoy the foliage and breathe clear Wisconsin air. A very happy birthday to Jim [her husband] on the 20th, presuming this letter makes it in time.

Sometimes I strike it rich at official dinners, in the sense of sitting next to a fascinating character who loves to tell stories and knows that I like to hear them. After Henry Chadwick's keynote address for the farewell to George Tavard last Sunday, we (around twenty guests) were wined and dined down by the river in a restaurant naturally called "Pier Three." I happened to lob right across from William Sessions, professor of English at Georgia State University, friend of such (now deceased) Southern writers as Flannery O'Connor and Walker Percy, of the Duke of Norfolk, of the editor of the *Tablet* [John Wilkins], and of others in England. (Last year his cousin, also William, had to give up being head of the FBI after serving in that post from 1987 to 1993.) Professor Sessions took Tavard at least once to meet Ms O'Connor who had to stay at home most of the time because of her mortal illness (lupus). Tavard is a very notable French theologian who spent much of his working life here in the USA, and is now retiring. Chadwick is an old friend of mine from Oxford.

The University of Notre Dame is performing badly at football: two losses and only three wins so far. They are the despair of the TV networks, as the team is followed (when successful) by millions of viewers. My love to you and all the family, Gerald.

Marquette University, Milwaukee, October 23, 1994.

My dear Moira and Jim, Thanks for your letter and the Melbourne Cricket Club memorandum. I have signed it and mailed it to them. Thanks for taking care of that.

Today (Sunday) the campus is very quiet, as many students

took off for a long weekend after their mid-semester exams. Yesterday I went about eighty miles along lake [Lake Michigan] to visit the chairperson of the department of theology, Pat Carey, wife (Phyllis), and their two teenage sons (Brian and Michael). They just took possession of a house (for weekends and the summer), the previous owner being the local psychologist. How much work a shrink would have in the lovely Wisconsin countryside beats me! But maybe the cold winters bring on problems. Or maybe I have it all wrong, thinking that city folk need therapy and country folk are all wonderfully normal and in touch with God, nature, their feelings, and everything else you are meant to be in touch with. Pat Carey, a church historian by trade and a very Irish American, has been extremely supportive and friendly towards me for years. It's thanks to him that I am enjoying this great study break in Milwaukee.

Small advance parties of Canada geese have started arriving. But the big flights are due in a couple of weeks. Some of the blighters have found city ponds in Milwaukee a good place for the winter; they let the others fly down to Louisiana and parts further south. Here in the city they strut around, crossing roads at will and tying up the nervous traffic. Next weekend I fly out to Claremont (California) to give a paper under the auspices of a philosopher friend, Steve Davis. We are planning a congress on the resurrection around Easter 1996.

A fair number of friends and acquaintances have been turning up in Milwaukee: Henry Chadwick (from Oxford), Thomas Halik (from Prague), Rod Strange (formerly at Oxford and then rector of the Beda College in Rome), and Paul Duffy, SJ (from Australia). Peace and love, Gerald.

Part III
Later Years of Pope John Paul II
(1995–1999)

Gregorian University, Rome, February 18, 1995.

[This letter refers to Giulio Andreotti (seven times Italian Prime Minister, now on trial for Mafia association and for murder), to John and Judy Brophy (friends from Sydney), and to Giorgio Barzilai (an eminent Italian engineer who carried further the work of Guglielmo Marconi and died in 1987). I celebrated the funeral Mass for Giorgio.]

My dear Moira and Jim, Thank you for your card from New York, and welcome back to the banks of the Yarra [the river that runs through Melbourne]—whoops, back to the mountains [their farm at Kilmore was on the crest of the mountains north of Melbourne]!

Here on the banks of the Tiber our second semester got under way last Friday. Around 225 in the class I am teaching on the doctrine of Christ (his person, natures, and saving work). There are seminars and other items to attend to; hence time is short for following the drama of the Andreotti case. But it looks as though they will nail the mafia connection on him. [They didn't; eventually Andreotti was completely acquitted of all charges.] John and Judy Brophy are in Rome; we lunch together on Monday.

I just recorded eight brief (two to three minutes each) reflections for BBC Radio Two. Do not fall into their hands; they are never satisfied. Having done work for radio since 1964, I thought I knew something about radio broadcasting, but that was an illusion. The BBC really does know better. The reflections go out from March 1, around 6.15 in the morning. I promised to do a little more for them later in the year.

Tomorrow (Sunday) I make my annual visit to Marino Laziale (not San Marino) to see Giorgio Barzilai's family, the older ones and the younger ones. Two weeks back I made a lightning visit to Venice to do a baptism. The city is as magical as ever, even at six in the morning when I was making my way through the fog to the railway station. Five years ago I officiated at the wedding ceremony for Donatella and Leonardo; later I baptized Francesco in Castel Gandolfo and now back to Venice to baptize Alessandro. Venice is the place for baptism and for everything. Much love to you and all the family, Gerald.

Gregorian University, Rome, March 12, 1995.

My dear Maev, Happy days in Canberra, Papua New Guinea, Melbourne, or wherever else this letter finds you. One way or another, I hope you will be celebrating with Moira on the 23rd [her birthday]. I did write to her, but please give her again my very best wishes.

A lovely spring day here in Rome. Despite the economic and political crisis, a good crowd turned out for today's marathon. Balloons went up and good cheer was exuded on all sides. Viva Italia! Viva Roma!

I did some bookings the other day for the summer. I leave Rome on June 29 for the USA and Oz [Australia], arriving in Melbourne (Jesuit Theological College, Parkville) on August 4. I leave for Perth and Rome on August 26. Four tulips have been blooming away happily on my window ledge for a week or more. No rough winds or heavy rain have done them in—yet.

Recently I did eight recordings, "Pause for Thought" for BBC Radio Two. The two producers, David Benedictus [a novelist and theatre director] and Jane Jeffes, [who later moved to Sydney and worked for the Australian Broadcasting Commission], did my technique the world of good. I now answer, or try to answer, the phone differently, being "allegro" one day, "allegro andante" another, "un po' melancolico" another, "commosso" another, etc. People will wonder what I am up to. But it's a way of practising my radio technique—at no cost. I'm warming myself up to record three or four pieces for Vatican Radio before Palm Sunday.

Several years ago an American seminarian (in first year) told me of dropping into an eating joint that was way out in the West of the USA. The radio happened to be playing and, even more remarkably, was tuned into the short-wave band for a Vatican Radio broadcast. He heard my voice! This confirmed him in his resolve to study for the priesthood in Rome, and lo and behold he hears the same voice (in thick Italian) reaching him in first-year theology, the first day of the first semester. It all sounded to me like a story Uncle Gerald [a Columban missionary in China for many years] might have told. I'm not sure what happened to the seminarian in question. But what a start!

I may have to go into radio silence over the next few weeks. The workload is "enorme," as the natives say around these parts. And I have to get some lectures ready for a Holy Week course I am to give in "Ammerdown," a retreat centre in Somerset. I went there several times from 1974 to 1985, but have never been back since. It's a most beautiful place, just a few miles from Downside Abbey and the lovely village of Mells, where Monsignor Ronald Knox, Horners, and Asquiths galore are buried. Peace and much love, Gerald. [Knox (d. 1957) was a notable Catholic writer; in the sixteenth century, Thomas Horner, celebrated in "Little Jack Horner," pulled out the pie by acquiring Mells Manor; Herbert Henry Asquith was British prime minister 1908–16.]

Gregorian University, Rome, April 8, 1996.

[This letter refers to the Australian journalist and novelist Desmond O'Grady, to a friend Mimi Sbisà and her husband Lee, to a Victorian Supreme Court judge John Batt, and to my barrister nephew Jim Peters.]

My dear Maev, The swifts are forming patterns over Rome, the Easter break has just opened, and it's about time that I write (before leaving to lead a retreat in England, April 10–20 down, or is it up?, in Somerset. The weeping Madonna of Civitavecchia fills the national newspapers ("They kidnapped the Madonna," bishop explodes) and gets good coverage as well on national TV. The Communist mayor of Civitavecchia has hired two ships to deal with the influx of pilgrims; magistrates have seized the statue pending further investigations (DNA tests on the tears of blood etc.), and the media continues to give the whole episode full and respectful hearing. The statue was due to be carried in a huge procession scheduled for Good Friday afternoon. Who knows whether the bishop will get the necessary court order and have the statue released in time for the procession?

My liturgical and para-liturgical functions seem tame by comparison. Last Sunday I baptized Giulia in the chapel of the Venerable English College. I had married her parents several years ago in the church of St Agnes (Piazza Navona). Why the chapel of the Venerable? Well, her mother had been baptized there thirty years ago, and her family has enjoyed all kinds of happy links with the College. So back we went. After I had filled in the books and put the vestments away, I stepped out into the Via Monserrato to ride around to their home (just off the Piazza Navona) on the back of the huge, red Honda that the father (Davide) drives (or do you say rides?). I felt the part, in my black suit and the vast helmet which Davide made me don. Sure enough, as we picked our way through the Sunday crowds strolling along the side streets, we ran into several Gregorian students, Americans who were rightly impressed by my daring. No chance of high speed, however, on such a short run down side streets Now I know what I was feeling when all those Harley Davidsons ripped past along the roads of Milwaukee when I was at Marquette University in 1993 and 1994.

Desmond O'Grady dropped by yesterday and gave me a copy of his latest, *Correggio Jones.* In a few minutes I'm off to an evening meal in the Castelli Romani, with Mimi, Lee, and a selection of the young folk. They will be pleased to learn that our book, *Friends in Faith* (Mahwah, NJ: Paulist Press, 1989) is to come out now in Portuguese, thanks to a publisher in Brazil. [The book expounded the Apostles' Creed, and drew on what thirteen young Italians had to say.]

I leave Rome on June 29, and via Newark, San Francisco, and Sydney reach Melbourne on August 4. I will be at Jesuit Theological College, Parkville, until August 26. A bit short, but I will have two weeks of lectures in Perth [at the University of Western Australia and elsewhere].

John and Margaret Batt will be here in early May. Young Jim appears [in court] before him now and then, and John is perfectly aware that he is dealing with my nephew. John and I got to know each other very well at Melbourne University, and have stayed in touch ever since. Much love, Gerald.

Gregorian University, Rome, May 11, 1995.

[This letter refers to my brother Glynn and his wife Barbara, to Peter Steele, an Australian Jesuit and poet, to an English journalist Mary Venturini, and to my nephew Stewart Peters.]

My dear Moira and Jim, Rome's streets are being swept, red carpets rolled out, and other last minute preparations have been taken in hand for the imminent arrival of Glynn and Barbara from the heartland of Tuscany. They stop only one night (May 12/13) and do so just beyond the Trevi Fountain. I am asking for a police escort to get me through the international mob of tourists who bring us to a standstill when we try to walk past the Trevi. It is our local fountain, and we of the Gregorian have a right of passage. What G. and B. don't know yet is that I will be loading them with a little post.

Did you notice some of the juxtapositions of names in the

index to *Experiencing Jesus* (London: SPCK, 1994)? Peter Steele, for example, next to Stalin and Iris Murdoch to Moses. The publishing house did the index themselves, but let me check it. It was interesting to find out what the anonymous index-maker wanted to put in, over and above the proper names I would have inserted myself.

Tomorrow my Californian friend, Dan Kendall, S.J., turns up for three weeks. We are working together on a book, *The Bible for Theology* (Mahwah, NJ: Paulist Press, 1997), having published six or seven joint articles. For the fun of it, we set out systematically to have articles in different journals: *Biblica*, *Catholic Biblical Quarterly*, *Gregorianum*, *Scottish Journal of Theology*, and *Theological Studies*. We haven't completely abandoned this "diversion," as we are about to put together an article ["Overcoming Christological Differences"] commissioned for a special issue (1996) of the *Heythrop Journal*. Dan is a great partner to research and write with. What he cannot find on his San Franciscan computer doesn't exist.

Next Tuesday the British Embassy to the Italian Republic is hosting a reception to honour Mary Venturini for the first ten years of her journal, *Wanted in Rome*. I used to write for it under the name of Stewart Peters and then send Stew a copy. For a while he thought (or at least pretended that he did) that there really was a Roman writer called "Stewart Peters." Mary V., by the way, is the one who joined me in co-authoring *Believing* (Mahwah, NJ: Paulist Press, 1991).

The new British Ambassador to the Holy See is a lady, not the first woman by any means to be an ambassador to the Vatican. But she is the first for the British Embassy *presso la Santa Sede*. She will keep me on her list: her underlings, who have been around for years, will see to that. Ambassadors come and go, but Pat (a secretary), David etc. stay on forever. David, by the way, is my favourite gorilla; he's the driver and body-guard of the ambassador. Lots of love to all the family, Gerald.

Gregorian University, Rome, June 2, 1995.

[This letter refers to my brother Jim and his wife Posey, Orietta and Frank Doria, other friends, Mimi Sbisà, her husband Lee, and Jared Wicks, an American Jesuit colleague at the Gregorian.]

My dear Maev, Thanks so much for your birthday phone call and letter. I'm so glad that the Indian slides [made by my Father in 1919] have gone to the National Library in Canberra. Please let me know if you can find anything further about Father's time in India [with the British army] from the office in London. Years ago I went there and started research on despatches, but ran out of time.

The day began well, with Italian jets screaming overhead and spewing out coloured smoke to form the Italian flag across the sky of Rome. Even if the second of June is no longer a fully operative national holiday as the Day of the Republic (people ask: Which republic?), they still do something to mark the occasion and, unwittingly, celebrate my birthday.

J. and P. are full of beans, and I am dying to hear Jim's report this evening from his medical congress on male impotence being held at the Vatican. Tomorrow evening (Saturday) I say a Mass for them and the Dorias in the Palazzo Doria—which seems to please Orietta [Doria] a great deal. This evening we are going to Castel Gandolfo to dine, chez Buccis [a restaurant overlooking Lake Albano], with Mimi and Lee.

Next week I head off to make my yearly retreat, this time in a Jesuit retreat house in Ariccia, right on the old Via Appia.

A very, very happy birthday on the 16th. I will have exams all day, but in the peace of the evening will raise a glass to you, in the company of Jared Wicks and other chosen souls. Much love, Gerald.

Gregorian University, Rome, September 26, 1995.

[This letter refers to Terry Waite, held hostage in Lebanon for a several years, and the Prince and Princess Doria Pamphilj, and their children, Jonathan and Gesine.]

My dear Maev, Enclosed are some items for you. The little folder on Blessed Dominic O'Collins [Irish Jesuit martyred in 1602] is meant for Jesuit breviaries. It was just published—a bit late [as he was beatified in Rome on September 27, 1992] but there you are. I thought someone in the family should have a copy. I hope this gets to you before you leave for Papua New Guinea.

Terry Waite has just done me a kindness by writing a foreword to the new edition of *The Second Journey*, about to be published by Gracewing, an English publisher. He didn't seem to mind my identifying his experience in Lebanon as a terrifying kind of second or midlife journey.

Next Saturday I have a wedding to "do" in St Agnes (Piazza Navona), with the reception to follow in the Doria Palace. Diana Korach (who lives in the Piazza Navona) has been a friend of the Dorias since she was a child; Jonathan and Gesine will be witnesses. Frank and Orietta are astonishing. Neither of them are well, and yet they keep on doing things for others. Much love, Gerald.

Gregorian University, Rome, December 3, 1995.

[This letter refers to my cousin Monica and her husband John, Desmond O'Grady (an Australian journalist resident in Rome), and John Wilkins (still very much the editor of the London *Tablet*).]

My dear Maev, A friend can carry this letter back to Australia to catch you before you leave for St Louis [for Christmas with our niece Marion Peters, her husband, and daughter]. My resolution for the New Year: stop criticising the Brits.

How can I be critical of them? They have been so good to me recently. The service of welcome for the Ruddocks (the new couple in charge of the Anglican Centre) was a delight. I was so pleased to meet Mark Santer (the Anglican bishop of Birmingham and an old-Cambridge hand) again. After the prayers we went across the Via del Corso for wine and chewies chez the Dorias. In a bookstore last week I ran into Fr Michael Beattie, an English Jesuit out in Rome with a group of his parishioners. "Why don't you come and stay with us in Farm Street [London] for a couple of months," he urged me. Bishop James O'Brien (an auxiliary of the Archdiocese of Westminster) and Bishop Jack Brewer (Diocese of Lancaster) had lunch, also last week, at the Gregorian. I managed to steer Jack Brewer towards the topic of the villa used by the Scots College up in Marino Laziale and how he encouraged a seminarian from Glasgow to describe their red wine as "Grotta Ferrata red." When we meet, let me explain the story. It has to be wired for sound to get the full-blooded effect [a Scots accent struggling with the "Rs" in Grotta Ferrata]. The British ambassador to the Holy See will have me back for dinner on December 11—to meet various folk, including a friend of hers from Belgrade. A good change, as sometimes dinners in Rome feature the same crew. Invite the usual suspects?

Yesterday, at 11 a.m., I went out to the baptism of the Dorias' second grandchild, Elisa. An excellent, young Roman priest, Don Luca, who is a friend of Gesine's husband (Massimiliano), performed the ceremony; then we crossed the Via del Corso to the palace for a drink. I had two negronis! My last negroni was years ago, with Fr Philip Caraman [an English Jesuit, writer, and unofficial chaplain to various famous authors like Evelyn Waugh], and both Philip and I had two. You ARE allowed a little break towards Christmas. Frank's hands were so cold, when I held them in my warm paws. The life is going out of him. Then in the evening I went back to say Mass at 7 p.m. for Frank and Orietta. He read the second lesson pretty well, but had little to say over the evening meal. They are so blessed by their butler, Mario, and Orietta is wonderfully brave and caring.

I leave for London and Cornwall on December 21 and return to Rome on December 31. Never miss the New Year on the banks of the Tiber? In London I will catch up with Monica and John, John Wilkins, and others. Desmond O'Grady is pretty cheerful; we talk once a week or so, and meet every now and then. Give them all in St Louis a big, Roman-Empire-size hug from me. Much love for Christmas and the New Year, Gerald. PS *America* magazine may carry an article by me in their Christmas number. [They did publish "Filling Our Senses."]

Gregorian University, Rome, February 5, 1996.

[This letter refers to a nephew Justin Peters, his wife Jill, a niece Joanna, and her husband Bob, the Australian journalist Desmond O'Grady, and Marcello and Vincenzina Mongardo, friends who lived in Umbria.]

My dear Moira, Thank you very much for your welcome Christmas gift and letter with all the news. I dropped a card to Justin and Jill when I heard of the arrival of Anna Catherine. Have a wonderful birthday on March 23 and then a GREAT wedding anniversary. You and Jim are an absolutely spectacular example of married life and family life for the whole, wide world. As the Italians say, *tanti, tanti complimenti!* I am sure the whole family will know how to celebrate the occasion as it richly deserves.

I doubt whether I will have time to write again in the next couple of months. The explanation follows. Tomorrow I fly off to Portland (Oregon) to give a couple of lectures; back to the Tiber mission on February 13. Then over to London February 23/24 to give one lecture at Digby Stuart College. Home at once to Rome. Then off again on April 1 (what better day for flying out?) to New York for the Resurrection Summit at St Joseph's Seminary, Dunwoodie. The proceedings I plan on calling "Resurrection Two Thousand." [In fact, Oxford University Press published in 1997 the papers as *The Resurrection: An Interdisciplinary Symposium on the Resurrection of Jesus.*] It is New York, after all, and one must think (and talk?) big. Still no final word on whether Luciano Pavarotti will show up to sing at the sacred concert [in St Patrick's Cathedral] on Wednesday, April 10. I will make sure of getting tickets to Jo and Bob for that concert. This may be the only way of seeing them, as the Resurrection Summit is being held a bit out of town, in Yonkers, and I really can't go awol [away without leave]. (Whoops! They will probably (certainly?) be out in Melbourne then?) I have to be back in Rome on April 11. Then no gadding around until June 25, when I move out for the summer: first the USA, and then Sydney (two days) and Melbourne (August 2–28).

Please say a prayer and light a huge candle in aid of Pavarotti turning up on April 10. I won't believe it until I see him there beefing out "I know that my Redeemer liveth," or something from Bach's Easter Oratorio, or an Easter hymn. If you ever see the journal *Inside the Vatican*, look for this month's number, and you will find something (thanks to Desmond O'Grady) on the Gregorian. *Newsweek* will have something (hopefully a cover story) on the occasion of the Resurrection Summit. I have known the religion editor, Ken Woodward, since 1967, and he is trying hard for the front cover. But, of course, such decisions don't come from him alone.

God is good, at least was so last Tuesday. I took off to Umbria for the day, visiting Marcello and Vincenzina at Foligno. Just a glorious, sunny winter's day, unlike the warmish but wettish days we have been having constantly. Marcello produces the best olive oil I have ever tasted. He gives me a bottle at every visit; it goes down well and rapidly at the International College of the Gesù. Much love to you, Jim, and all the family, Gerald.

[Pavorotti did not come; for the full story of the Resurrection Summit, see G. O'Collins, *On the Left Bank of the Tiber* (Brisbane/ Leominster: Connor Court/Gracewing, 2013), 290–91. The scholars who shared in all four Summits (1996, 1998, 2000, and 2003) were: Sarah Coakley, Stephen Davis, Stephen Evans, Dan Kendall, Carey Newman, Gerald O'Collins, Alan Padgett, Gerard Rafferty, Alan Segal, and Marguerite Shuster. Others who attended one or more Summits included: Jean-Noël Aletti, William Alston, David Brown, Caroline Walker Bynum, Shawn Copeland, Brian Daley, Gordon Fee, Francis Schüssler Fiorenza, Robert Kiely, Brian Leftow, Kathleen Norris, Peter Ochs, Pheme Perkins, Janet Martin Soskice, Eleonore Stump, Richard Swinburne, N. T. Wright, and Linda Zagzebski,]

Gregorian University, Rome, March 4, 1996.

[This letter refers to a Sydney friend, John Brophy, to my brother Glynn, to Desmond O'Grady, an Australian journalist, to a friend who lived at Castel Gandolfo, Mimi Sbisà, and her husband Lee, to her son Matteo, and daughter-in-law, Marina.]

My dear Maev, I can hardly imagine the glee of John Brophy over the results of the national elections in Australia. [John Howard replaced Paul Keating as Prime Minister.] You must have phoned him, or maybe he phoned you. Please congratulate Glynn from me on winning the Seniors Championship once again [at Metropolitan Golf Club]. Poor Mike Fitchett, his old time rival! Thanks for the Australia Day fax.

Because I don't live in Australia, they threw me out of the Australian *Who's Who*. But I have been creeping back elsewhere, and hope that we are alongside each other in the *Who's Who in Australasia and the Pacific Nations* (3rd edn just published by the International Biographical Centre, Cambridge, UK).

Desmond is off shortly for a month in Australia, and showed me a copy of a lecture he will be giving on Australian feelings about living in Italy. I have been gathering memories for him, ones that convey something of my wonder and affection. Recently (on a Sunday) I went up by the little train to Castel Gandolfo. After lunch with Mimi and Lee, I headed back to Rome on the same little train, but had left my return ticket behind in the copy I gave them of *Wanted in Rome*—something I discovered shortly after boarding and just before the ticket collector arrived. "I had a return ticket," I explained in my best Italian. "But I left it behind in a newspaper at Castel Gandolfo." He shrugged his shoulders and went off down the train. In what other country could I have done that and had such a response? Yesterday I took a walk past the Colosseum and back to the Gregorian via the Circo Massimo. On the Via dei Fori Imperiali, a tourist party trotted by in an old horse-drawn carriage. The driver was talking to someone on a mobile phone. It just seemed weirdly incongruous.

Two cultural items appeal to me enormously: first, the way Italians telephone at 7.30 in the morning to plan the day. You may not make appointments ahead of time. They must be made or at least confirmed earlier the very same day. My fantasy is that half of Italy phones the other half at 7.30—to arrange their schedules day by day. As you know, Italian babies are much loved and cared for. I get fascinated by them when they are lying in a pusher, bound or rather encased in an excessive amount of clothing, their arms and legs stuck sideways, and their wonderful eyes swivelling around to pick out passers by. As I go past, our eyes often meet, and I fancy all kind of great messages get communicated between the bambini and myself. Maybe they are practising very young for that extraordinary eye contact and swivelling vision of the grownups, especially the grownup males.

Don't miss a number of *Newsweek* that comes out around March 30. Mimi, by the way, is a grandmother: Ludovica, born a month ago to Marina and Matteo. Much love, Gerald.

Gregorian University, Rome, April 28, 1996.

[This letter refers to Davis McCaughey, the governor of the State of Victoria 1986–92, and his wife Jean, Don Vincenzo Paglia (who promoted the canonization of Oscar Romero, and became Archbishop Paglia and President of the Pontifical Academy for Life), my sister Dympna, my cousin Monsignor William McCarthy who restored St Patrick's Cathedral, Melbourne, in time for its centenary in 1997.]

My dear Moira and Jim, Congratulations on your 50th wedding anniversary. I gather the party was simply superb, not to mention the speeches. Davis and Jean McCaughey will be here in ten days time, and I look forward to dining with them (on Jean's 79th birthday, as it happens). Today (Sunday) I was over in Trastevere for the lovely baptism of Ludovica, the first child of two friends. The parish priest of Santa Maria is simply all heart. I couldn't wish for a better p.p. in the lives of Matteo and Marina, whose home is just a few hundred yards from the basilica. Good on you, Don Vincenzo! Naturally the buffet lunch starred any number of veterinarians, as both Matteo and Marina are in that field. But there were a few others to spice things up, like the Portuguese interpreter of the current Italian President (Scalfaro). As we came out of Santa Maria, I ran into the former President (Cossiga), who also highly approves of Don Vincenzo and comes every Sunday to a particular Mass in the basilica.

On Friday last Jean Vanier gave a talk at the Gregorian on the movement he founded to care for the handicapped, L'Arche. He has very deeply touched and changed the lives of some of my friends. After hearing him, I understand why.

Five weeks of term to go, then exams, then off on June 25 for the USA and Australia. I reach Sydney on July 31, jet-lagged out of my mind by the non-stop flight from Los Angeles. After visiting the aunts in Sydney, down to Melbourne on Friday August 2, arriving on QF423 at 11.20 a.m. Any plan yet for a big bash on Dympna's birthday [July 31]? I am sorry that the schedule of lectures in the USA doesn't let me arrive in Melbourne for the day itself.

Bill McCarthy wrote recently to invite me to give one of the lectures for THE celebration. I will speak some time in 1997. So I will be looking for suggestions please when I arrive this coming August. [The lecture, "In Praise of Cathedrals," was published in *America* magazine, November 20/27, 1997.]

I noticed the other day that the Australian *Bulletin* (for April 8) carried the *Newsweek* piece (also published on April 8) by Ken Woodward on the resurrection. A quick glance seems to suggest that everything was the same, except for *Newsweek* putting on the cover a fine picture [actually of Jesus' transfiguration] by Raphael. Much love, Gerald.

Gregorian University, Rome, May 26, 1996.

[This letter refers to James Peters and his wife Sally, and to Moira's eldest daughter, Marion, and her husband Rick.]

My dear Moira and Jim, Thank you very much for your birthday gift, which will be put to good use. The idea of a night at your home on August 2, to celebrate Dympna's birthday before she leaves sounds excellent. Whatever and wherever, I am free. On the morning of August 2, I will be coming in from Sydney, and would like to touch base over lunch with the Jesuits at the Jesuit Theological College in Parkville where I will be staying. But in the evening I can be free. Great to hear that Sally and James will be giving you another grandchild [Marion Jennifer Peters] in the spring. Please pass on my congratulations.

Today (Pentecost Sunday) I was out at the English College villa on Lake Albano with a group of Italian friends—for our annual Mass and picnic together. This time was highlighted by a good number of little ones: Pietro and Ludovica (only three or four months old); Francesco two years and a bit; Piergiorgio four or five; Margaux ten going on eleven. There is a wonderful garden for them to play in, and a couple of them took to the swimming pool.

Classes end this week; exams start (for me) on June 8. In the meantime loads of institutions and people want to hold dinners: the British ambassador to the Holy See; the English College; my painter friend, Giuseppe Crescimbeni, etc. I am here until June 26, then off to the USA, spending most of the time at the University of Notre Dame [South Bend, Indiana]. Then onto Sydney after a weekend in St Louis with Marion and Rick (July 27–28). Much love, Gerald

Gregorian University, Rome, August 27, 1996

My dear Jim and Moira, It was wonderful to catch up with you both again—in the afterglow of your 50th wedding celebration. Thanks for the excellent party for Dympna and for the lunch at the Windsor Hotel. As always, I was very happy to catch up with many of your grandchildren, their spouses, and the grandchildren. They are an indispensable part of my life.

Moira, thanks for seeing me off at the airport. It gets me away to a great start on the road back to Rome. Much love, Gerald.

Gregorian University, Rome, December 1, 1996.

[This letter refers to Kate, the older sister of my sister-in-law Posey, Dan Kendall at University of San Francisco, Steve Davis at Claremont College, and my nephew James Peters and his daughter Marion.]

My dear Moira and Jim, It was GREAT to hear from you and have all the news. On Saturday November 23, I said the Mass and did the funeral for the wife of Desmond O'Grady, the journalist whom you read now and then in Australian papers. She died suddenly in her sleep. R.I.P.

As I said, I leave Rome on December 22 and after a couple of days in London, go down to Kate & Co. in Cornwall. I will be back at the Roman base latish on December 31. Not too late though, as it is better to be home on New Year's Eve than out on the streets. I normally try for a flight out of London around 2 p.m. But by late October all the earlier flights were full. The good news, though, is that British Airways has given me a free flight Rome/London/Rome. My annual mileage just manages to cover one or two such free flights.

Loads of snow in Northern Italy, rain here in Rome, but the weather is still reasonably warm. Next Saturday I will be up in Umbria for the day, visiting Marcello and Vincenzina Mongardo, who live in Foligno but spend a good deal of time in Trevi, a village just down the road from Spoleto. Both are retired school teachers, and are wonderfully interesting folk, who are full Europeans. Nothing like an Italian who is European- or even world-minded.

Lots of exciting ecumenical items this week: the discussion at the Vatican on papal primacy (with Henry Chadwick from Oxford, Mike Buckley SJ from Boston College etc.); then quite by chance (or providence?) Archbishop George Carey [Archbishop of Canterbury] and his wife Eileen arrive today or tomorrow for a quick visit to the Pope and Cardinal Joseph Ratzinger. They go on to Milan later in the week. I urged the Careys to see whether Cardinal Carlo Maria Martini could take them to the opening night at La Scala, which should be next Saturday night.

A few years ago Queen Elizabeth talked about her "annus horribilis." November 1996 to September 1997 is turning out my "annus mirabilis" or even "excessivus" for publishing: *Focus on Jesus* (Leominster, UK: Gracewing, November 14, 1996), *The Resurrection* (Oxford University Press, April, 1997), and *The Bible for Theology* (Paulist Press, September 1997). The first and third I wrote with Dan Kendall; the second was edited by Dan, Steve Davis, and myself. The only "downside" in the whole scene is that Gracewing and OUP don't supply the copies for relatives and friends that come from Paulist Press.

My love to all the family and happy birthday to James on December 12. I am dying to see baby Marion; Posey told me that she is an utterly beautiful baby. Peace and love, Gerald.

Gregorian University, Rome, March 9, 1997.

[This letter refers to the Australian Cardinal Edward Cassidy (who was President of the Pontifical Council for Promoting Christian Unity, 1989–2001), and to my niece Joanna Peters, who lived in New York with her husband and two children.]

My dear Moira and Jim, It is a gorgeous, sunny day in Rome, high time that I wrote to wish you a very happy Easter. I leave here on Monday March 24 for Somerset, returning to Rome on the late afternoon of Thursday April 3. So I will be off your radar screen for a while. Near Bath I will be leading a Holy Week retreat at a centre called "Ammerdown," looking at the daffodils, listening to the cuckoos in the woods, and, at the end, giving a young Oxford University graduate a bit of help in his career as a journalist. Presuming that Cambridge University wins the boatrace on Saturday March 29, I might find that Alex has disappeared into the woods to commune with nature and to cope with his sorrow at the dark blues's loss. [Cambridge, the light blues, won by two lengths.]

An Australian TV group (Channel Nine) arrives next weekend, and will give me a good chance to show my face again at home. It's for a program called "Getaway," aimed at tourists, as you know or can guess. I will try to inject a little old-time religion into it. They are going to shoot in Rome, Florence, and Venice. I want to get in a little dig against the Florentines by taking the TV group to the cloister where Michelangelo was originally buried (in a Franciscan convent just a few yards from the Gregorian). Some Florentines sneaked in at night and nicked his body, which is now awaiting the general resurrection up in the Church of Santa Croce in Florence. Only a few yards from this convent is the palace where the Stuarts lived in exile: Bonnie Prince Charlie was born and died there. We can shoot that palazzo as well. Will that scene tell for or against Australia's decision to become or not to become a Republic [a reference to the national referendum on November 6, 1999, which was not carried]?

Tomorrow I will phone again to see whether Cardinal Cassidy will show his face on Channel Nine and, even more importantly, whether he will dress up in red. The "Getaway" people want him, and they want him in red.

I have already booked my flight for June: on Sunday June 15, I arrive in Melbourne at 8.10 a.m., but will then need every moment of sleep and quiet after that, in order to get ready for the BIG LECTURE on June 17 ["In Praise of Cathedrals" to be delivered at St Patrick's Cathedral]. I have asked the Jesuit Theological College for a room.

A very happy wedding anniversary on April 6, and a very happy birthday, Moira, on March 23. If you are talking with Jo, please give her my best for March 18 [her birthday]. I had a great visit with them in New York last month, but forgot their birthdays. Every blessing and grace at Easter. Much love, Gerald.

Gregorian University, Rome, November 23, 1997.

My dear Moira, Jim, and your delightful sons, daughters, outlaws, and grandchildren, As I am off to Cornwall on December 20 (returning to the Tiber outpost on December 30), this has to be the Christmas letter. This last week brought teams of visitors and a couple of book launches to fill up empty moments. On Monday just over fifty students from the several-months-long course at Bossey, an ecumenical institute outside Geneva, turned up to spend the morning here and let us (i.e. some professors and students) fill them in about theological education in Rome. They were from all over the world and included the daughter of Bruce Barbour (an old friend of mine who runs the United Faculty of Theology out of an office at the back of Queen's College, Melbourne) and an Irish Presbyterian who shares numerous friends and acquaintances with me. On Thursday, John Wilkins, the editor of the London *Tablet*, came to supper. He is in town for two weeks covering the first half of the American Synod, held in the Vatican. John seemed impressed that I had been invited to bury Richard Mason, the author of *The World of Suzie Wong*. "It had quite a cult-following," he commented. Secretly

I wondered: "Is it doing anything nowadays for the image of Hong Kong?" At table he joined some Jesuit scholars who had just arrived from Pune, Boston, Frankfort etc. They are to evaluate the Gregorian academically. Will we get top marks? Or will they push for a whole new team of professors? Or both? Here's hoping.

Last Monday afternoon a mega book-launch brought two cardinals, several bishops, many professors, mobs of students and phalanxes of other well-wishers together for the *Festschrift* (nearly 1000-pages long) in honour of a Spanish theology professor who has just turned 70. Angel Anton (how would you like to be called "Angel"?). Even after a Neapolitan [Bruno Forte] spoke for around an hour and others had commented on his work in teaching ecclesiology (check in your dictionary please), Anton could still respond vigorously and at length. The whole performance lasted nearly three hours. These are the shows that keep us young here in Rome.

On Saturday afternoon, I spoke at another book launch, *Toward a Christian Theology of Religious Pluralism* [Maryknoll, NY: Orbis Books, 1997] by Jacques (I call him "Jim") Dupuis. A good crowd but lacking ecclesiastical heavyweights. Only one bishop (who spoke) was present [Bishop Michael Fitzgerald of the Pontifical Council for Interreligious Dialogue]. Admittedly there was a spectacular concert going on at the same time up at the Vatican, as well as some other competing items, like the president of the German bishops' conference telling his audience in the "Teutonic College"—yes, that's what it's called—how valuable it is to study in Rome. I always knew that Bishop [later Cardinal] Karl Lehmann was an intelligent and discerning person. Incidentally, he should have been appointed Cardinal Archbishop of Cologne, but he looked too liberal to some of the Vatican worthies [and remained for years as Bishop of Mainz]. Anyway back to Jim Dupuis and religious pluralism. The fact that I first met him in the foothills of the Himalayas over 25 years ago, and went around on the back of his motorcycle (alas an inferior Yugoslavian machine and no Harley Davidson) to visit a Buddhist monastery, a Tibetan refugee camp run by the sister-in-law of the Dalai Lama, and the mountaineering school headed by Tenzing Norgay gave me some lively stories to spice my appreciation of Jim's excellent opus. Much love for Christmas and the New Year, Gerald. [A Tibetan Sherpa, Tenzing in 1953 joined a New Zealander Edmund Hilary in the first proven ascent of Mt Everest.]

Gregorian University, Rome, March 5, 1998.

[This letter refers to my niece Joanna and her two children, Ken Woodward (religion editor of *Newsweek*), and Aunt Mary Lewis who lived in Sydney.]

My dear Moira and Jim, Please give my love to Joanna, especially on her birthday (March 18), and to Adelaide and Douglas. I hope they have a GREAT visit and will also be around, Moira, for your birthday on the 23rd.

We are heavily into the second semester, and it brings some other chores: such as the dialogue with a group of Japanese from Tenrikyo (next Monday through Wednesday). They are a religious group founded in the last century, and have many attractive features—not least their stress on joy. On the occasion of their visit, the Gregorian will be featuring an exhibition of documents and other items from early Christian activity in Japan.

Until after Easter, I may not be able to write again, as the Trinity Summit (Easter in New York) is consuming all my free moments. With God's grace and Ken Woodward's help, *Newsweek* will run a cover story on the Trinity in their Easter number. The Holy Trinity doesn't need our publicity, but the book to emerge from the Summit will be helped by any such publicity.

The Irish and Irish sympathizers are gearing up for the BIG feast (St Patrick's on March 17). Celebrations open on March 12 (the reception at the Irish Embassy to the Holy See) and continue for a week or so. Talking of the Irish, I referred a young, engaged couple from Western Australia to the Irish College, where many Saturdays they run a kind of marriage factory. Couples who want to avoid large and expensive celebrations at home come and get quietly married in Rome. The bridegroom from Perth phoned me out the blue yesterday afternoon. "Where better to get married in Rome than the Irish College," I told him, and passed on the fax number of the College at once.

Yesterday I lunched at the Gregorian with a priest from Nepal. Afterwards we went up on the roof and let our eyes run across the Roman skyline. "You see so many churches here," he remarked. "In Kathmandu we look over hundreds of temples."

You must know that Aunt Mary turns ninety on April 13, Easter Monday. Happy wedding anniversary and Easter, Much love, Gerald.

Gregorian University, Rome, May 31, 1998.

[This letter refers to Sir James Gobbo, who was still governor of the State of Victoria, his wife Shirley, my brother Jim, and his wife Posey.]

My dear Maev, Thanks for the phone call, the first for my birthday, and thanks for your gift which shall be turned into some liquid asset. GREAT news about the Australian Catholic University; I hope and pray that this comes off as expected. [She was to be appointed an adjunct professor of ACU]. A very happy birthday on the 16th.

Visitors are pouring out of the skies these days. On Monday last, Jim and Shirley Gobbo arrived and we had lunch together. He will receive an honorary doctorate at the University of Bologna tomorrow, the penultimate day of class here at the Gregorian, which effectively blocked any chance of my joining him. On Wednesday a certain Patricia (plus several in her entourage) came from London; she is a visionary and since the 1980s has been receiving visions and locutions from Jesus and his Mother. The topic centres on the millions of aborted children and the possibility of their being officially recognized as virgin martyrs. Shortly after she left, John Cornwell walked across from the Hotel Eden to take me off to lunch. He was back in Rome from Cambridge (UK) to do more work towards his biography of Pope Pius XII [the sensationalist and unscholarly *Hitler's Pope*]. John published a work on visions etc. several years ago, *Powers of Darkness, Powers of Light*. But I thought it best not to distract him by telling him about Patricia.

On Friday a senior American widow, Betty Voli, turned up with a bunch of fascinating, 18th-century letters from a young Roman nobleman, Virgilio Cenci, who took three years on a trip to Paris, Madrid, and London. She wants to publish an English translation of them.[8] After she went, Gavin D'Costa dropped by. An Indian, he teaches at the University of Bristol, and has been a visiting professor at the Gregorian the last six weeks. I provided the last instalment of his salary and an icon of three angels visiting Abraham and Sarah—not the familiar one by St Andrew Roublev but one that features Abraham and Sarah much more prominently. Gavin, Beryl, and their two little children return to Bristol late this week. To round things off, a Polish priest, Marian, flew into Rome on Saturday and came at once to visit me. He is writing a doctoral thesis on my views about divine love and the resurrection. After an hour or more he departed happily (with a book and several offprints under his arm), and I left to say Mass for the Dorias. All systems are go for the visit of Jim and Posey, who should be arriving at their hotel any moment now.

On June 30, I leave Rome for a month in the USA, mainly at the University of Notre Dame to teach in their theology summer program. I return to Rome on August 6, and leave again on August 14 for the Jesuit community at Marquette University, Milwaukee. Much love, Gerald.

Marquette University, Milwaukee, September 16, 1998.

My dear Moira and Jim, All is well in Marquette, even if steam is drifting up from a deep hole outside my window. A firm that supplies us with steam (for heating and hot water)

---

8   On her behalf, I contacted the venerable London publishers, John Murray, who were famous for publishing that kind of work. John Murray VII replied and expressed his regret that times had changed; he could not publish the Cenci letters. In 2002, Hodder Headline took over John Murray.

has finally located the leak, and will fix it on Tuesday. If the whole contraption blows up in the meantime, please invent something witty for my tombstone: wafted to God, melted by divine love, died in the heat of the moment, in his element at last, went to a steamy grave, inspired as ever! See if you can come up with something better.

Yesterday a representative of Augsburg Fortress lunched with us. An agreeable person, Rod Olson is visiting faculties and seminaries up and down the country to keep us all aware of the good things Augsburg Fortress, traditionally a Lutheran firm but now very ecumenical, is publishing (around fifty titles a year). I think he was amazed at how many publishers I know and some of them quite well.

Tomorrow night, the President of Marquette, Fr Bob Wild, is taking me to a symphony concert. Hooray for a little culture! Life is so busy in Rome that, as you know, I can do little in the cultural direction and sometimes feel like one of the damned in Dante's *Inferno*. Food is very, very close, but hideously just out of reach.

Along the corridor from me in the Jesuit residence is Fr William Kidd. Now I would have thought that in the USA any parents called Kidd would never, never call their darling son William, just as in Australia no parents by the name of Kelly would christen their little boy Edward. Or have the times changed? [I was thinking of the outlaws, Billy the Kid and Ned Kelly.]

Here at Marquette, the Clinton critics are full of beans. I haven't bought a copy of the *Starr Report* [an investigative account by independent counsel Kenneth Starr of the US President, Bill Clinton, which had been released on September 11, 1998].

The media are over the top, keeping the public watching and reading. The whole thing has rather spoiled Rafter's victory for me. [The Australian tennis player Patrick Rafter had just won the US Open.]

In November I'm spending a weekend in La Crosse (to the west of Milwaukee) with Bernie McGarty, a parish priest who has been behind everything I have ever done in Wisconsin, either in Milwaukee or in Madison [for a conference on St Augustine in the fall of 1991]. He was in town the other day for the funeral of a hundred-year-old aunt, and at once invited me to come and preach for him. He is going to lay in quantities of *All Things New* [Mahwah, NJ: Paulist Press, 1998] and have me sign them for his parishioners. Curiously I know some of them already, even without having ever set foot in La Crosse, the Steingraebers [stone diggers/cutters]. Despite that ominous name, they are very lively and in no way remind me of cemetery dwellers or workers. The bishop of La Crosse, Ray Burke [later Cardinal Raymond Burke], is a former student of mine and old Roman hand.

Please pass on my love to all your children, their spouses, and grandchildren. I feel badly not being able to write to one and all. But to console myself I am putting them (and the two of you) into an account of my life and times in Rome that I am writing [*On the Left Bank of the Tiber* (Brisbane/Leominster: Connor Court/Gracewing, 2013)]. So far Stephen, Bronwen, Mark, and James have made their appearance in the text. I want to prove to readers that it is fun being visited in the eternal city by nephews and nieces, especially if they are called Peters. Much love, Gerald.

Marquette University, Milwaukee, October 11, 1998.

[This letter mentions a Canberra priest, Julian Wellspring, whom I came to know during his studies in Rome, and Dan Kendall, SJ, from the University of San Francisco.]

Dear Maev, It was good to hear about Julian's ordination, as well as about the conference on Pacific Representations. Next Thursday (October 15) I fly over to Boston and give a lecture at Boston College, returning to Marquette on October 17. But the important date is Monday October 19, when a young friend of mine, Fr Greg Mustaciuolo, is going to the Metropolitan Museum with Cardinal O'Connor for a meal. He hopes to persuade the folk at the Metropolitan to put on an exhibition of paintings and sculptures featuring Jesus right around Easter 2000, so as to coincide with the Incarnation Summit that Steve Davis and I have organized for Easter 2000 in New York, the last of these "summits" I hope. [It wasn't. We did one more in 2003, the Redemption Summit.] I'm praying that the Cardinal and Greg, his private secretary, can pull this off for us. It would be nice to end the series of three New York Summits (1996, 1998, and 2000) with a bang. [In fact, at Easter 2000 the Metropolitan hosted a lecture by David Brown (then of Durham University) on Christ's humanity and divinity in twentieth-century art, followed by a reception for the seven hundred invited guests around the pool of the Egyptian Temple.]

This morning I attended the eight o'clock Mass in the Milwaukee Cathedral to enjoy hearing Archbishop Weakland preach. The Mass is broadcast on the local radio every Sunday, and I can understand why. He preaches in such a lively fashion, and the liturgy is done with dignity and joy. I had only a word with him afterwards, but hope to see him with more leisure during these months at Marquette. [His retirement in 2002 would be overshadowed by the news that, years before, he had conducted a sexual relationship with a male associate, and that $450,000 had been paid to settle litigation arising from the affair.]

The Episcopalian chaplaincy at the University of Chicago invited me to talk about Anglican-Catholic relations on October 29. So I will do that, visit a gallery or two, and rush back on October 30, as Dan Kendall comes in for a weekend here. He has a so far undisclosed project. I strongly suspect that he has in mind to publish something in 2001 to mark my 70th birthday. Good on you, Dan. [What he had in mind became D. Kendall and S.T. Davis (eds), *The Convergence of Theology: A Festschrift Honoring Gerald O'Collins, S.J.* (Mahwah, NJ: Paulist Press, 2001).]

Apropos of Anglicans, the Archbishop of Canterbury [George Carey] wrote the other day to see whether I might manage to write his Lent Book for 2000. I hastened to agree. It has to be something on Jesus—for the millennium year. The publisher is HarperCollins; so at many removes I will be working for Rupert Murdoch.

Have a GREAT launch on the 14th. I think Grandfather's letter stands a fair chance of being read to all and sundry at the party. Much love, Gerald. [I was referring to Brenda Niall and John Thompson (eds), *Australian Letters* (Melbourne: Oxford University Press, 1998), and Grandfather's letter of 1897 proposing marriage to our Grandmother, Abigail Dynon. The book was launched in Canberra by David Marr, a friend of Thompson, who was then head of the Australian studies section of the National Library of Australia. Now retired from Papua New Guinea to Canberra, Maev attended the launch].

Marquette University, Milwaukee, December 1, 1998.

[This letter refers to Steve Davis, professor at Claremont McKenna University, California.]

My dear Moira and Jim, Please excuse this style of Christmas bulletin. But it's all I can manage. This letter is coming off my personal computer at Marquette University in Milwaukee. Once again the Marquette Jesuits invited me to be the Wade Distinguished Professor in the department of theology (August–December 1998), a chair which I also held back in 1994 and which involves little more than running one seminar for graduate students. The campus is a mile or so from the immensity of Lake Michigan, which—if you didn't know—is bigger than all of Switzerland. Long ago beer made Milwaukee famous. In those good old days every kitchen in the city was reputed to have three taps, labelled hot, cold, and Schlitz. Nowadays the Miller brewery is still located there, but great names like Pabst (and, I think, Schlitz) have become extinct. The big keg has shifted to St Louis, the headquarters of Anheuser-Busch. Milwaukee may be like Chicago three million people ago, but the 600,000 locals think, read, and talk. So the four months have let me do lots of writing, which has included finishing two books: *The Tripersonal God* (to be published by Paulist Press in 1999) and *The Trinity*) (to be published by Oxford University Press in May 1999). The latter volume, in collaboration with twelve others, emerged from the Trinity Summit, which I co-chaired with Steve Davis last Easter in New York and which brought together biblical scholars, theologians of different stripes, and philosophers. My excuse for all this writing (and I haven't listed everything by any means) is that it's a practical way of showing effective gratitude to Marquette for providing wonderful facilities and opportunities. Mentioning and thanking the University in the introductions might provide a little more publicity for what is any case a very stimulating place to pursue theological studies at the graduate level.

Before coming over to Milwaukee, I preached in Westminster Abbey on August 2, and afterwards met several students from the Gregorian. You cannot escape from them, no matter how hard you try! These ones were studying English in London over the holidays, saw the notices about evensong in the Abbey, and came along to give me moral support. Anther service that did my spirit good was a superb organ recital given by Mary Beth Bennett in the historic St Patrick's Church of Washington, DC. She was celebrating not only the Solemnity of Christ the King but also the Feast of St Cecilia, which this year fell on the same Sunday (November 22). I had flown down to Washington to give a brunch talk for 200 members of the John Carroll Society. The pastor [a friend from Rome, Peter Vaghi] scheduled my visit, so that he could launch locally my latest, *All Things New* (Paulist Press), a spiritual book offering a little inspiration for Advent, Christmas, and the New Year. Naturally the publishers and author were glad to collaborate.

On December 11, I head home to Rome and my normal address at the Gregorian University. I will spend the Christmas and New Year period reading theses, before taking off for a week (January 17–24) to lead a retreat. After that, except for Easter, when I lead a Holy Week retreat at Ammerdown (in Somerset), I will not stir out of Rome until the very end of June 1999. As we move to Christmas and another year, may our loving God bless you and all your dear ones. *Buon Natale e felice Anno Nuovo.* Love to you both, as well as to all the family, Gerald.

Gregorian University, Rome, February 7, 1999.

[This letter refers to Moira's youngest child, Steve, and his fiancée.]

My dear Moira, Thank you very much for keeping me up to date about Marianne and Steve. They are dears, and I look forward hugely to their wedding. As I said, I am here in Rome (except for a week in Somerset over Easter) until the end of June; then to the USA, flying out to Sydney/Melbourne around July 15 (from San Francisco, of course). Then I plan to be in Oz until the end of August, which will make a quick visit to Singapore for the wedding more than possible.

Examinations are in full swing at the Gregorian, but not having taught during the first semester, I have only a little to do: some comprehensive boards to man/person next Thursday and Saturday morning. On Wednesday I go to Florence for a day, mainly to hear a lecture by the Irish President, who will be speaking at a meditation centre housed in the lovely, Benedictine monastery of San Minato. Various local worthies like the Cardinal of Florence will be there at the lecture and, presumably, at the lunch which follows. Mary McAleese then heads for Rome and a meeting with the Pope. She may be meeting the Archbishop of Canterbury [George Carey] at the same time and place (Rome or perhaps even the Vatican). He is due into Rome on Friday to bless and inaugurate the new Anglican centre, housed as before in the Doria Palace but in a much finer apartment now, after thirty years in one that could only be described as a country vicarage.

A couple of days ago an English friend, now British vice-consul in Chicago, sent me a postcard about a visit home to the UK to help her mother leave the old family home: "She is now in a nursing home and very happy; she has a lovely gentleman friend. She was 89 on Wednesday. He is 98 and really clear. I am very happy for both of them." That has to be the most cheerful letter or postcard I received last week.

By some blessing and grace I don't deserve, yesterday I managed to finish the ms. of *Following the Way*, the Archbishop of Canterbury's Lent Book for 2000. Once a friend has read the ms. and passed on some suggestions, I can incorporate them and send the work off to HarperCollins, the English publisher who will also have an American outlet—hopefully not HarperSan Francisco, their counterpart in the USA which has a very mixed catalogue of books. The A. of C. asked me to do this book late last year, and I could get to the actual writing only from December 17. No, I'm not the first Roman Catholic or Jesuit to do a Lent Book for the A. of C. Tom Corbishley, SJ, did one back in 1973.

A very happy birthday on March 23, in case I don't get to write before then. Things are going to get incredibly busy again from next Wednesday. Much love to you, Jim, and all the gang, Gerald.

Gregorian University, Rome, March 3, 1999.

[This letter refers to two friends from Sydney, John and Judy Brophy, and to my niece Joanna.]

My dear Moira, Life is about to turn even more unbelievably busy in the next three weeks. Hence this early birthday letter. Very happy returns on March 23. I will be over in England, leading a Holy Week retreat, away from Rome March 29 until April 9, and flat out getting it [the retreat] ready the previous week.

Right now Rome is plastered with signs of a political meeting scheduled for next Friday and featuring Gerard Collins, the Irish vice-president of the European Parliament. Now it's bad enough having a journalist (who also writes for the *Tablet*) called Gerard O'Connell also living in Rome. Someone wrote recently to ask whether anyone had ever seen him and me together in the same room. This week I have been explaining repeatedly that I don't lead a double life in the European Parliament. The general public runs together much too easily O'Collins, Collins, and O'Connell. Come on, folks, give the O'Collinses a break.

On Sunday last I had a magic Sunday lunch with the widow of Richard Mason, author of *The World of Suzie Wong*, whom I buried in the Protestant cemetery in October 1997—near Keats and other notables. Maggie has been wanting to offer me a Sunday dinner by way of thanks, and she had wonderful company for the occasion. They included Peter Rockwell, third son of Norman Rockwell, and like his dad an artist, although more of a sculptor than a painter. At 62 or 63 he is still trying to get over being Norman Rockwell's son. At the same time he is planning a cover for *Wanted in Rome* [the paper co-edited by Maggie]: it will feature Bernini peering into the skull of an art critic, trying to figure out what the fool is up to. Another guest, a journalist whom I know well, regaled us with the story of the landing in Red Square of a small aircraft flown by a crazy, young German pilot. Franco [Venturini] was there and, of course, faced the problem: "Shall I run the story?" He told us of an American dentist who filmed the whole landing (on the bridge and then taxiing into the square to be greeted warmly by the guards who all thought it was part of a media stunt), offered his film to one US network for a $1000, only to have his offer turned down but then picked up instantly by another network.

John and Judy Brophy phoned yesterday; they are in town for a busy week, but I will have a meal with them tomorrow. Please give Joanna my best for her birthday on March 18. Much love to you and all the family, Gerald.

Gregorian University, Rome, May 23, 1999.

My dear Maev, A marvellously sunny day here in Rome for Pentecost. Charismatics arrived en masse yesterday, and I hope that their prayers will bring a renewed outpouring of the Holy Spirit on everyone in the eternal city. We need it.

A very, very happy birthday on the 16th. It is still more than three weeks off, but I wanted to make sure this letter reached you before you leave for Papua New Guinea. I hope your ex-students and other friends up there put on a fantastic celebration or two for you. I will be starting examinations that very day: 180 or so orals, 65 or so written exams. But it will be the first day, and I will certainly be fresh and strong enough to raise a glass to you at lunch.

Do you remember Bill Burrows, a Society of Divine Word priest who taught at Bomana [the seminary outside Port Moresby in Papua New Guinea], left, and became some years ago the head of Orbis Books (just outside New York)? You (or someone else?) took me up to Bomana in the 70s. Burrows turns up tomorrow and will take Jacques Dupuis and myself out for a meal. It is the least he can do for old Dupuis, whose latest book has come under fire from the Holy Office, and is now into a paperback edition with Orbis. [Cardinal] Ratzinger and Co. really boosted the sales of the book, which came out simultaneously in English, French, and Italian at the end of 1997. I have enjoyed acting as Dupuis's consultor. It's a somewhat uneven encounter, which Ratzinger stretches language to call a "dialogue." They hold some power, but show a gross lack of theological competence in the charges they have brought against Dupuis. He wrote (and then sent them in January) a marvellous 180-page reply to their charges, a reply that could be adapted and become a useful book, as a fine summary of his original 433-page book. I must suggest that tomorrow to Burrows.

Last Tuesday I had an evening meal with Jonathan and Gesine Doria, the first time the three of us have ever sat down together by ourselves. In a way that was most moving they talked about their parents, Frank, who died last October, and Orietta, who battles along with cancer. I wrote part of Frank's obituary for the *Tablet* and, with help from Jonathan and Gesine, am putting together one for Orietta. As I leave Rome on June 28, spend a couple of weeks teaching in the USA, and then six weeks or so in Melbourne, I want to have the text ready and approved by J. and G. before I leave the banks of the Tiber and the sheltering walls of old Rome. Once again, a very GREAT birthday. Much love, Gerald.

Part IV:
The Last Stretch
(2000–2006)

Gregorian University, Rome, September 1, 2000.

Dear Moira, Thank you once again for seeing me off in such fine style for London and Rome. Here is the form from the Melbourne Cricket Club which was waiting for me when I returned last night to the Gregorian.

It was wonderful to find you looking so well. We all need you so very much—just for being what you are, the loving, encouraging head of the whole family.

A mountain of letters to answer now. Much love, Gerald.

Gregorian University, Rome, November 13, 2000.

[This letter mentions an Australian journalist, Desmond O'Grady, and Mikhail Gorbachev, president of the USSR 1988–91.]

My dear Moira, Jim, and all the family, Yesterday at lunch with Desmond O'Grady we finished the meal with some panettone, that wonderful brand from Milan, "Tre Marie."

Never have I eaten panettone so early in the season—a week or two before Christmas, yes, but never just over six weeks before Christmas. Yet I interpreted it all as an invitation to get cracking on my end of the year correspondence. There are two doctoral defences bearing down on me, loads of classes, visitors galore, and the usual round of seminars and meetings.

I had hoped to escape writing a piece for the Christmas issue of the London *Tablet*, but Annabel Miller was on the phone the other day urging me to submit an article. Whether it makes the grade and gets published by them is another question. I first wrote for the *Tablet* at Easter 1968!!! Surely I deserve to be pensioned off by now? Give me a break, Annabel, will you! In short, I must write for Annabel and send you a letter now or never, before leaving Rome on December 21 for six days away in a parish. So a very happy and grace-filled Christmas. [I did write and publish an article for the 2000 Christmas issue of the *Tablet*: "The King and the Maiden."]

Today Gorbachev is turning up at the Gregorian to give a lecture at an international meeting on peace. The only catch will be for the poor students trying to make it through the security and attend their regular lectures. But maybe the students will feel like Ethel Turner in her *Ports and Happy Havens*: "We have walked with the gods! We have been to Rome!" The text should be changed to: "We have walked with Gorbs!"

The Scots College students performed wonderfully well in welcoming the Queen on her visit last month to Rome. But now they insist on celebrating vigorously their 400th anniversary. Any excuse for a party? At all events I must front up to a BIG celebration on St Andrew's Day.

This is all to share with you a little news but lots of love for Christmas and the New Year, as well as warning you that I will be away from Rome December 21–27. Much love, Gerald.

Gregorian University, Rome, January 6, 2001.

[This letter refers to Mark Coleridge, at that time working in the Vatican's Secretariat of State and now Archbishop of Brisbane.]

My dear Moira and Jim, A few hours ago the Jubilee year closed officially, on a mildly sunny Saturday morning with maybe 150,000 at the Pope's Mass in St Peter's Square. I watched a little of it on TV; that square is a superb setting for people working for television. If they mess up a transmission from a place which offers them an Egyptian obelisk, a Bernini colonnade, a Michelangelo cupola, and the rest, they should throw themselves into the Tiber at once.

Tomorrow the Roman mayor, Francesco Rutelli, who helped immensely to make the whole year a raging success, resigns and sets about his campaign to become Italy's next prime minister. Here's hoping! He is pitted against Mr corrupt, money-bags Silvio Berlusconi, who has been putting out propaganda for months now. Anything you can think of— family life, care of nature, etc.—Berlusconi says that he is for it. Really? No, I'm not showing my prejudices. But we Italians gave Berlusconi one shot at being prime minister, and it ended miserably. Why should we make the same mistake again? [Berlusconi was re-elected and served as prime minister 2001–2006, and later from 2008–11.]

I must pass on to you two discoveries of mine. The first concerns James Walston, the son of a famous (American) mistress of Graham Greene. Walston teaches for an American university here in Rome. I would love to ask him what he thinks of *The End of the Affair*, Greene's story (now turned into a film for the second time) of G.'s affair with Ma Walston. But a question along those lines would be more than indiscreet. However, if JW wants to volunteer any remarks, G. O'C will be all ears.

You may nor may not remember the Ostrogoths. They were bad news, perhaps not as bad as the Huns and the Vandals, but still bad news in our parts. On the Roman subway system there has been a sign: "If you want to, you may speak Ostrogothic to the driver. But please do so courteously."

Last Tuesday Mark Coleridge and I went out to have a delightful evening meal with Desmond O'Grady, Marina [Desmond's cook], Marina's son (Tommaso), and Raffaella, a multilingual Italian of about 40 or 45 who publishes facsimiles of famous manuscripts. Yes, I said famous. I think she worked on a facsimile of the Codex Vaticanus (fourth-century Bible). Now Desmond told me that she had recently married a 70-year-old. But he was not in evidence. Or was he? Is he Desmond? Who knows really? And it doesn't matter. [It wasn't Desmond.] What matters is that the occasional lunches and dinners chez Desmond, with Mark always in cracking form, are about the most relaxing times I can imagine. Relaxation ends on Monday January 8, with the return of the students.

A case that your most capable son James helped me with is about to end, amicably I hope. I must tell James how much he contributed to the solution. I have a letter all ready to go off to the London *Tablet* to put the best (and truest) light on the document that the Congregation for the Doctrine of the Faith [CDF] intends to publish. (I saw it in advance.) Anyway young James must take much credit, training his uncle as an advocate. A very happy birthday to Jill [their daughter-in-law] on the 21st and to Stewart [their eldest son] on the 3rd. Much love, Gerald.

[The closing paragraph refers to the action of the CDF against Jacques Dupuis, which involved a meeting with the CDF on September 4, 2000 (at which, coached by James Peters, I spoke for the defence) and reached a partial closure with their "notification" (about Dupuis's book *Toward a Christian Theology of Religious Pluralism*) of February 26, 2001. See the *Tablet* for March 3, 2001, which used my letter to state the significance and limits of this notification; for a full account, see my *On the Left Bank of the Tiber* (Brisbane/Leominister: Connor Court/Gracewing, 2013), 213–51.]

Gregorian University, Rome, February 11, 2001.

My dear Moira and Jim,

[This letter refers to the family of Giorgio Barzilai, a dear friend who died in 1987 and whose funeral service I conducted in his parish church, Marino Laziale.]

I am writing this in Rome, but will post it in London later this week, when en route to Cambridge and a little preaching at Fisher House, the Catholic Chaplaincy. I return to Rome on Monday February 19—in time to start the second semester and, of course, to share in the big celebrations of the 44 new cardinals. A great start to the second semester! At least half of the seven new ones to whom I wrote a letter of congratulations are younger than yours truly. At least Cardinal Avery Dulles is older, thank God, 13 years older to be exact. As he both taught at the Gregorian and took his doctoral degree here, we are holding a reception and hosting a meal for him at the Gregorian. Another twelve or so of the new cardinals are alumni, but they will have engagements elsewhere, in their old colleges etc.

On Sunday January 21, the day when the Pope read out his list of 37 new cardinals,[9] I went to the Capranica College for Mass (starting at 11.30) and the lunch that followed—all in honour of that seminary's patron saint, Agnes, whom they love very much. Several archbishops and bishops (all of them old-boys of the Capranica) concelebrated with Cardinal Ruini [the Pope's vicar for the diocese of Rome], himself an old-boy. When the Mass ended around 12.45, the Rector thanked the Cardinal, the choir, etc., and announced that the Pope at high noon had just created a new bunch of cardinals, including Archbishop Pompedda, one of the concelebrants. There was a fairly modest bit of applause at that news. I couldn't help thinking that if the Capranica had been the North-American College, the applause would have lasted for ten minutes. In fact, as I learned quickly at the pre-prandial drinks, there was another old-boy among the new cardinals, but the lads of the Capranica had hoped that they would have three old-boys on the list of new cardinals! They were a little disappointed.

Among the guests for the dinner was Senator Giulio Andreotti, seven times Italian Prime Minister, and much *contestato* [a controversial person]. Whatever you say about him, he seemed to be right at home, "a good friend of ours," the seminarians assured me. I got myself photographed with him, so that I can document our historic meeting. We talked

---

9   The following Sunday he added seven more to the list, notably, Bishop Karl Lehmann of Mainz, whose omission from the first list triggered widespread negative comment.

about using CDs for research on Thomas Aquinas, if you are curious about the nature of our conversation.

Today I was up at Marino for lunch with the young Barzilais. Sabina and Marco now have two fine young boys, Ian and Luca. You will meet some of them at the big party on Friday June 1 [a celebration anticipating my 70th birthday, which was to take place on June 2]. Giorgio had three children married when he died, but only two grand-children, and now there are six. Much love, Gerald.

Gregorian University, Rome, March 18, 2001.

[This letter refers to Desmond O'Grady, an Australian journalist who lived in Rome, and to my niece Joanna and her daughter.]

My dear Moira, Today, the Sunday within the octave of St Patrick and Joanna's birthday, I put on my brightest green sweater—to be honest, my only green sweater—to walk across Rome to take a tram and then a bus to lunch with Desmond O'Grady. Italians young and old were out in large numbers for a late morning walk in the spring sunshine. They have the city looking clean and splendid.

Joanna will like the new look. She arrives tomorrow with Adelaide, for a week of sightseeing in and around Rome. Addy has never been here before, and I don't think Jo has visited the city since the 1970s. Some friends of hers have been in Rome shooting a film [*Gangs of New York*] directed by Martin Scorsese, and Jo promises to take me to the scene of action [the studios at Cinecittà on the edge of Rome]. The film stars Leonardo DiCaprio. In the last few days he has been sighted in the Doria Gallery. Jonathan Doria refused to bother the poor guy, and insisted that he be left alone to enjoy Caravaggio, Velázquez, and the rest.

A very happy birthday on the 23rd and a very happy wedding anniversary on April 6.

On Palm Sunday, April 8, I fly to London and will lead a Holy Week retreat down in Somerset, at Ammerdown, a centre where since 1974 I have led eight retreats, all but one of them in Holy Week. I return to Rome on the evening of Thursday April 19. A very happy and blessed Easter to you and all the family, and much love to you and Jim [Moira's husband], Gerald.

[During their stay in Rome, Scorsese's (fourth) wife had a baby, which I offered to christen. But they preferred to postpone the baptism until they returned to Brooklyn from Rome.]

Gregorian University, Rome, April 22, 2001.

My dear Moira, Last Wednesday the service of thanksgiving for the lives of Frank and Orietta Doria, held in the chapel of Lambeth Palace [London], with a reception following in the Guard Room, reminded me forcefully of the film, *Chariots of Fire.* So many gallant, older folk attended, like Henry and Peggy Chadwick from Oxford and Owen and Ruth Chadwick from Cambridge, not to mention all the British Ambassadors to the Holy See, from Sir Mark Heath on. Jonathan Doria read the first lesson, and I read the second. The Archbishop [George Carey] preached wonderfully well. Princess Margaret was to come, but was stopped by another (small) stroke. Cardinal Cormac Murphy-O'Connor also was sad not to be able to attend. There were so many oldies I had met in Rome, from the 1970s on, who have returned to live in England.

After leading a retreat near Bath, I was able to stop overnight in London—en route back to Rome and the frantic weeks at the end of the second semester. Please put in your diary the following dates: I leave Rome on June 27 to lecture in the USA, and spend a weekend with Joanna [in New York]; on July 17, I arrive at the Jesuit Theological College in Parkville [Melbourne]; then on August 23, I leave for Singapore and, after a few days [of lecturing], return to Rome. In haste but with much love, Gerald.

Gregorian University, Rome, November 12, 2001.

[This letter refers to Cardinal Edward Cassidy, who was about to be succeeded by Cardinal Walter Kasper as President of the Pontifical Council for Promoting Christian Unity, to Kate, the sister of my sister-in-law, and to my niece Joanna.]

My dear Moira and Jim, In a few days I am picking up my ticket (for London/Washington DC and back to Rome), and am feeling that work, other appointments, and visitors are rushing me through November and into December so that it is now or never to write to you for Christmas and the New Year.

Cardinal Cassidy is back from Australia and in Rome for two more weeks. I hope to catch up with him, before he finally leaves Vatican Hill for Newcastle [Australia]. Anglicans galore have been or will be coming and going, not least for next Friday's installation of Bishop Richard Garrard as the new director of the Anglican Centre (in the Doria Palace). An old pal from Cambridge days, Bishop Geoffrey Rowell, will visit Rome to install Richard. A little later in November, Archbishop Peter Carnley [Perth, Australia] will spend a few days at our Casa del Clero [near the Piazza Navona] and take part in an Anglican-Roman Catholic meeting.

On December 20, I leave Rome for London, just in time to catch the Christmas reception offered by the *Tablet*. John Wilkins turns 65 that day. I will miss him when he retires as editor in a year or two. Over Christmas I will be down in Cornwall, with Kate, Sarah [her eldest daughter], Justin [her son-in-law], and the rest. Please God my wellingtons, or rather the wellingtons they bought for me several years ago, are still there in the laundry. Cornish mud, especially in the winter, has to be seen to be believed.

After Christmas I fly to Washington, DC, to preach for my old friend, Monsignor Peter Vaghi, at St Patrick's, a downtown church. If possible, I will slip up to New York and see Joanna before flying back to Rome on the evening of January 6. On the 6th, a Sunday, Cardinal Avery Dulles will be down from New York to celebrate a big Mass for Peter, and I get to preach as well as keeping my eye on Uncle Avery (now 83) at the altar.

The line of Rosemary Dobson [Australian poet] about life being "an ebb and flow under the distant stars" keeps running through my mind, in connection with a little flow on my behalf to take place on November 30. That evening in Velletri an international centre for "Borgia Studies," in collaboration with the city council of Velletri and the local rotary club, are going to award me the "Stefano Borgia" European prize for 2001–2003. Yes, Stefano was a very distant relative of Lucretia and Co., but lived later, in the 18th century, a person of culture who kept Velletri on the map. It is also the city where San Geraldo, a bishop of Velletri, is buried. I haven't been there to pay respects at his tomb since 1974, and this is my chance to do so again. By the way, Lucrezia's nephew, St Francis

Borgia, joined St Ignatius Loyola in being the co-founder of the Gregorian University. Much love to you and all the family, and every Christmas blessing, Gerald.

[On November 30, at the same ceremony, Chiara Lubich also received an award. I helped to promote her for the 1977 Templeton Prize for progress in religion and peace. Founder of Focolare Movement, she died in 2008; the cause for her beatification was formally opened in 2013.]

Gregorian University, Rome, March 3, 2002.

My dear Moira, Hooray! Hooray! I was delighted to learn that your problem [an operation for cancer] appears to be behind you. At least that is what seemed to be the news from the family. In any case, a very happy birthday on the 23rd. It may be a Saturday, but it is the last day of class for me before the Easter break. I volunteered to teach on Saturday morning, as it keeps down the numbers who follow the course; those who come really want to take the course. So I shall celebrate the 23rd with more gusto.

Gesine Doria's great dane is a joy to take a walk with. You cannot believe how many people I met yesterday on our little trot over to the Piazza Navona. I am getting a new image in Rome, even if Roldano clearly thinks of me in one way only: "He's the chap who takes me out for a walk."

I am in Rome until April 2, and then fly out to give two lectures in New York [for Aldo Tos in Greenwich Village]. I hope to see Joanna [her daughter], and I hope also to have finished by then a book I have been writing for years: *Catholicism* for Oxford University Press. They asked me, and I agreed. So keep your faith until you read this book, written with blood, sweat, and tears. One curious feature is that the seven advisers for OUP, all anonymous, obviously want the book and want it to be as good as possible. Some of them, via OUP, sent me many pages of suggestions. God bless them, but it makes for more work.

Last Tuesday I went to the Approdo Romano ("Roman Landing") to hear a lecture by the outgoing British Ambassador to the Holy See on relations between Britain and the Holy See since the sixteenth century. Mark Pellew spoke (in Italian) so well. The audience was marvellous. Members of the Approdo Romano include Alessandra Barberini, Philippe Casanova, Orietta Machiavelli, Luciano Grimaldi (see the royal family of Monte Carlo) etc. The etc. includes the president, Paolo Boncompagni Ludovisi, who is descended from Gregory XIII, a pope who married before he took holy orders, and then as pope was an enormous benefactor of my university, hence named the Gregorian University.

On June 27 I leave for the USA, and arrive in Parkville (Jesuit Theological College) on Thursday August 1. I will be there for most of August. Peace and love to you, Jim, and all the family, Gerald.

Gregorian University, Rome, March 6, 2003.

[This refers to my niece Joanna who lived in New York.]

My dear Moira, The best of birthdays on the 23rd. May family and friends gather around and let you see how much we love you and treasure you. I will be giving a lecture that Sunday morning to the members of the American parish in Rome—on the resurrection. It will be the first in a series of three Sunday presentations on the resurrection, the other two being given by much younger members of the Gregorian's staff: a German and then an Irishman. Philipp [Renczes] and Tom [Casey] are very bright and charming. I am glad to be the first, as I could be an anticlimax if I followed them.

This semester I teach a class on Saturday morning (for two hours) to 130 students, and run a seminar on Friday afternoon (also for two hours) for 13 students. Since both the course and the seminar deal with doctrines about Christ (e.g. his incarnation, resurrection and saving work), the Friday afternoons and Saturday mornings dovetail nicely.

Before the proofs of three books—yes, three: one written by myself, one in collaboration with a colleague, and for the third I am a joint editor—hit my desk, I am moving ahead with a book on Vatican II that I am writing with John Wilkins, the editor of the London *Tablet*. He will cease being editor this year, after more than twenty years in the office; I think he rather likes the idea of having a "retirement" project already under way. [In the event I was the sole author of *Living Vatican II: The 21ˢᵗ Council for the 21ˢᵗ Century* (Mahwah, NJ: Paulist Press, 2006), but the book was dedicated to John and he contributed some expert editing].

The dinner and overnight at Joanna's (April 24/25) are prepared, with the guest list already available. I will have just finished the Redemption Summit on the outskirts of New York, and will move to Washington on Friday the 25ᵗʰ, and fly back from there to Rome on Sunday 27ᵗʰ. Jo has Mike Hausman, the producer of *Gangs of New York*, with his wife Pam, coming to dinner. She has also asked the local parish priest, Aldo Tos, a wonderful Italian-American who has been pastor for years in Greenwich Village. Much love to you, Jim, and all the family, Gerald.

Gregorian University, Rome, March 30, 2003.

My dear Moira and Jim, A very happy wedding anniversary on April 6. I shall raise a glass to you at a meal with John Kennedy, a lay headmaster of Loyola College [a high school], Watsonia [suburb of Melbourne], who will be visiting Rome with his wife that weekend. I cannot remember whether he is a relative of the great Hawthorn football player [Australian rules]. Years ago I did ask him that question, and I have forgotten his answer. I will ask again.

Last night I had supper with Desmond O'Grady and enjoyed a piece (on the making of saints) he has written for an Easter issue of *The Sydney Morning Herald*, which presumably, if accepted, will also appear in the Melbourne *Age*. On April 1, I say a funeral Mass in Santa Susanna's church for Maureen Cobban, the wife of the Australian Ambassador to Italy who died in Rome eleven days ago and was buried in Canberra. Tuesday's service will give Roman friends and acquaintances of the Cobbans the chance of some delayed prayer and celebration.

By the time you receive this, a Christian/Muslim dialogue will have begun in Qatar (!!!) on Sunday April 6 and will have been in the news. The Emir (God bless him) has invited various Muslim thinkers and leaders and some Christians like Archbishop Rowan Williams [Archbishop of Canterbury], Fr Dan Madigan, SJ, and Professor Frances Young [University of Birmingham] to share in a symposium—all as his guests. Talk about dialogue right on the front line! Dan is an Australian

Jesuit, who teaches and works at the Gregorian in interreligious dialogue. Frances was a fellow doctoral student with me in Cambridge [UK] in the 1960s; she married a doctoral student (not in theology) who was with me at Pembroke College. When the meeting ends, Dan is flying to Turkey for some further engagements. I hope his airspace is safe.

On April 14, I leave for a couple of days in Oxford (to talk with Oxford University Press about publicity for my *Catholicism*— to appear this coming September), and then on to New York and a meeting on redemption (fairly relevant nowadays). I will stop with Joanna overnight, and then go down to Washington to preach, returning to Rome on April 28. A very blessed and happy Easter to you both and to all the family. Much love, Gerald.

Gregorian University, Rome, October 6, 2003.

[This letter was sent to my brother-in-law, Jim Peters, on the occasion of his 90th birthday.]

Dear Jim, A very, very happy birthday on October 20. I will be in Rome, recovering from the beatification of Mother Teresa of Calcutta the previous day. I will be working with the BBC, who are covering the ceremony; so you might see me doing that. You will have a delightful celebration; my warm thanks for being such a wonderful brother-in-law and friend. On the 20th I will say Mass for you, Moira, and all the Peters family.

On October 21 I leave for San Francisco to do a little lecturing for the University of San Francisco, before flying back to Rome on November 30. Once again a very wonderful birthday celebration. Peace and love, Gerald.

Gregorian University, Rome, April 1, 2004.

[The letter refers to my deceased brother Glynn, who was born April 1, 1934.]

My dear Moira and Jim, What better thing to do on Glynn's birthday than write a few letters, to you and others? I am around for Easter Sunday, leaving only for a few days chat with folk at Oxford University Press (April 13–18). British Airways has given me a free flight to London for the occasion.

Visitors drop out of the Roman sky constantly. Last week began with forty Finns, Lutheran pastors and their spouses, who wanted to be filled in about matters Catholic and Lutheran. Then there was an American couple whose wedding I did 33 years ago; they are still cheerfully together and are grandparents several times. Australian bishops on their ad limina visit swarmed around Rome, and on March 24 I joined them at a Mass in St John Lateran's, which was followed by a reception in the Irish College [almost next door to the Lateran Basilica]. A great friend and benefactor [Dr Eugene McCarthy] was in town from New York; he has funded two chairs [in theology and philosophy, respectively] at the Gregorian and flies over for the major lectures of the current chair-holders. George Carey [former Archbishop of Canterbury] has been occupying this visiting chair in theology, giving an optional course on ecumenical affairs. But for his major, public lecture, George spoke on Islam and Christianity, and, thanks to a reporter from the *Telegraph* stirred things up in the news circles of London and made the media outlets in Australia.

For some peculiar reason God keeps me in good health. Does the Trinity require more books from me? Right now I am towards the end of writing a work with John Wilkins on living the Second Vatican Council [see letter of March 6, 2003]. After that? Yes, there are other items coming or at least planned. The Vatican II book will be published by Paulist in 2005 [actually in 2006], as part of a series they have organized to coincide with forty years since the Council closed. I am in Rome till June 29; then in the USA, and reach Parkville [Melbourne] on July 15. With much love to you and all the family, Gerald.

Gregorian University, Rome, May 26, 2004.

[This letter refers to my nephew Stephen, and his wife and daughter.]

My dear Moira and Jim, I hope Maev realizes that her birthday [June 16] is a very special day this year, as it is the centenary of Bloom's Day in Dublin (1904–2004). The Irish will be celebrating accordingly. [June 16, 1904 was the day of action for Lionel Bloom in James Joyce's novel *Ulysses*.]

On June 29, I leave Rome for London (a lunch-hour talk for a Christian group in the House of Lords, no less) and then on to Newark, New Jersey. I will give some lectures in a course for priests, and hope to catch up with Joanna plus Douglas and Adelaide [her children] and the Browns [the parents-in-law of my niece Marion; they lived in New Jersey]. Then on to San Francisco (July 11–13), then to the Jesuit Theological College in Parkville [Melbourne], arriving Thursday July 15 at 7.55 a.m. after a fifteen hour flight from Los Angeles. On Saturday August 7, I leave for Thomas More College, Perth [to lecture at the University of Western Australia]. From there to Singapore (August 30 until September 5) to give some lectures and, of course, catch up with Steve, Marianne, and

Samantha. You might let them know that I am coming. I think that I am staying with Les Raj, SJ, [in the Jesuit parish], but that is still to be confirmed.

This is a heavy social time in Rome, with visitors from the USA and Australia, a dinner with the baby Dorias [Jonathan and Gesine Doria], a Queen's Birthday reception [at the residence of the British ambassador to the Holy See], doctoral defences, and lots of other items. In a few minutes I go downstairs to hear a visiting professor [Eleonore Stump from St Louis University] on the stain of evil according to Thomas Aquinas. Much love, Gerald.

Gregorian University, Rome, October 26, 2004.

[This letter refers to Giulio Andreotti, seven time prime minister of Italy.]

My dear Moira, I hope Jim's birthday was a roaring success. As you know, I was over in Washington to lecture at Georgetown University and enjoy being back at the scene of the wedding [of my niece Marion Peters; see above the letter of April 4, 1983]. Two young friends, British journalists (she writes for the *Telegraph* and he writes for the London *Times*), live in Georgetown, with their two boys. It was wonderful catching up with them and being able to attend a family Mass with little Joe and Ben.

Rome is getting ready for next Friday's signing of the European Constitution, with parts of the city blocked off and some flights in and out of the two airports to be cancelled. Presumably the signing explains the visit of the Taoiseach [Irish prime minister] and a dinner being offered in his honour by the Irish Ambassador to the Holy See. Yes, I was asked, but I felt bound to decline as I go on retreat Friday morning. On the phone the secretary at the embassy agreed that Jesus should take precedence over Bertie Ahern.

Last week was so full of engagements, that going on retreat seems pure bliss. There were two congresses at which I delivered papers: one on the face of Christ at the Urban University (where I had Giulio Andreotti curled up in the front row facing me) and the other on Pierre Teilhard de Chardin [Jesuit palaeontologist], which provided the occasion for my first appearance on French television. They are preparing a documentary about him, in view of next April being the 50th anniversary of his death in New York. The Teilhard fans began in Rome their series of congresses to mark the anniversary: the meetings will take them to Paris, Cairo, China, England [all places where he lived], and, finally, New York. I have never known such a series of celebrations to mark the 50th anniversary of anyone's demise. But Teilhard deserves it. I told the French public (as my opening remark for the TV interview) that I much prefer Teilhard's Christ-centred view of history to Voltaire's idea that history is "a tableau of crimes and misfortunes."

For good measure, a crew making a film for Italian TV turned up as well last week, and wanted me to talk about Dan Brown's *The Da Vinci Code* and Mary Magdalene. If you happen to watch CNN, you can see me on a CNN special about the Madonna and Mary Magdalene (to go out around December 10). A very agreeable, youngish man from New York, David Gibson, is the producer of the special. That is enough TV for the time being, but I was glad to get back in front of the cameras to prove to myself that I could still perform at least adequately.

Last week I had a meal with Jonathan Doria, who had as his guests his house-master (plus wife) from Downside Abbey school. Austin and "Mo" (I have no idea what her real name is) still live near Downside, which puts them near Ammerdown, where I will be preaching a retreat at the very end of 2005. The retreat house should look much grander then, as it is being renovated drastically. The first time I went to Ammerdown was in 1974, and I keep saying "this is my last appearance." But I keep going back to lead courses or retreats there. Somerset is a very special part of the world. Much love to you, Jim, and all the family, Gerald.

Gregorian University, Rome, November 24, 2004.

Dear Moira, Jim, and all the Peters family, Thanks very much, Moisie, for all the communications around the time of Dympna's [our sister's] death and funeral. I appreciated that very much and was most grateful that she had a wonderful send-off, and only sorry not to be there myself.

After appearing live with BBC world television on the occasion of Mother Teresa's beatification in October 2003, radio and television dropped out of my life. I was beginning to think that the media folk had decided en bloc that I was over the hill. But now they have come back strongly. If you see CNN at all, you can catch me on a special program to go out around December 10, on Mary and Mary Magdalene. Every Thursday/Friday I now have a few minutes on an English broadcast of Vatican Radio. Next March, ABC's "Foreign Correspondent" [Australian Broadcasting Commission] will do a special on the *Da Vinci Code*; they recorded my observations last week. The DVC was also the theme of some remarks I recorded for an Italian program ("Enigma") that will be aired on December 27. French television wanted me to talk about Teilhard de Chardin; they are doing a program for the 50th anniversary of his death (April 2005). I contrasted the views of history expressed by Voltaire and Teilhard, and added: "I prefer Teilhard." Next week Radio Scotland turns up to record maybe something on the DVC, or maybe on another topic like studying and teaching in Rome. So whatever else is happening, I am back in the media doing something I enjoy, not least because it is good practice for teaching.

On January 2, I leave for London and then some days of lecturing in Washington, DC, returning to Rome on January 12. Much love to you and all the family at Christmas and the New Year, Gerald.

Gregorian University, Rome, June 11, 2006.

[This letter refers to a dear friend from Melbourne, John Batt; he and his wife flew in from Australia to celebrate my 75th birthday and departure from Rome.]

Dear Maev, Here is our schedule. Monday June 12, we are both invited to dinner by Tracy Wilkinson and her husband. I think his name is O'Connor. She is the *Los Angeles Times* correspondent in Rome, and is writing a book on exorcism. We are due at 8 p.m., and their apartment is within walking distance of your pensione. What if I arrive at your pensione around 7.15; we can have a chat and then walk around to their apartment.

Tuesday June 13: party with Gesine Doria and her husband Massimiliano Floridi, plus 35 others, including Dan Kendall

[Jesuit friend from San Francisco]. I can come to your pensione around 7.30, and we can wander off to the Doria Palace.

Wednesday June 14: reception at the British Embassy to the Italian Republic, in honour of the Queen's Birthday. I can come around at 6.30 and we head there together.

Thursday June 15: Irish College reception hosted by Mary Wilsey [Venturini] and Maggie Mason [editors of *Wanted in Rome*]. It starts at six; so I had better be there by 5.45 or so.

Friday June 16: 8 p.m. dinner at the Abruzzi restaurant, very close to the Gregorian. Our waiter is nicknamed "il principe delle tenebre (the prince of darkness)."

Sunday June 18: twelve o'clock at the Gregorian, for lunch with John and Margaret Batt. [The rest of the letter is lost.]

Marquette University, Milwaukee, August 31, 2006.

My dear Moira, Greetings from old Milwaukee, where Marquette University has resumed lectures, and I am happily running a course on redemption for eleven graduate students in theology. The weather is still fabulous, even if there is the slightest touch of fall chill in the evening air. The campus is very beautiful, a downtown situation, just before you enter the city centre and move on to Lake Michigan.

Most of the Jesuits in the residence where I am staying (slap in the middle of the campus) are friends from my previous stints here (occupying the same visiting chair) in 1994 and 1998. One has the glorious name of William Kidd ("Billy the Kid?"). In Milwaukee itself the breweries are mainly gone (taken over and shifted to St Louis and maybe elsewhere), or rather turned into museums. There used to be a saying that every house in Milwaukee had three taps in the kitchen: hot, cold, and Schlitz.

I am organizing a couple of trips to Washington, DC, or rather "they" are doing so: a quick overnight in September to give a lecture on Jesus (who else can I talk about?) at the Foreign Press Club, and then a longer visit (five days) in November (to give a lecture and lead a seminar at Georgetown University) and receive an award (the Johannes Quasten Award for Excellence and Leadership in Religious Education and Research) at the Catholic University of America. Quasten was a great German scholar who taught at CUA into the 1980s.

I struggle along writing the next book, a study of other religions [*Salvation for All: God's Other Peoples* (Oxford: Oxford University Press, 2008)]. Happy days and much love to you, Jim, and all the family, Gerald.

November 2006.

My dear Moira and Jim, Every blessing to you and all your dear ones at Christmas and for the New Year. Let me sketch my situation. I have left (yes, left for good) the Gregorian and from mid-December will be living in a Jesuit community in Wimbledon for two years. After consultation with the Australian Jesuit provincial, I accepted an offer from St Mary's College, Strawberry Hill (University of Surrey) to be a research professor with them for at least two years (December 2006 to December 2008). The campus of St Mary's is about twenty minutes by train from Wimbledon.

Right now I am finishing a semester as a visiting professor

at Marquette University and fly to London on December 14. Please give all your children and grandchildren my love, Gerald. PS I get to Australia around July 20, 2007.

Part V:
Letters to Jane Steingraeber
(1995–2013)

[The fall semester of 1994/95 I spent as Wade Professor at Marquette University, Milwaukee (Wisconsin). A friend of mine, Monsignor Bernard McGarty, helped to bring about that invitation, which would be twice repeated (1998/99 and 2006/07). By inviting me in the fall of 1994 to cross the State of Wisconsin and lecture in La Crosse, Bernie shared with me a number of his local friends. They included Jane Steingraeber, who taught nursing at Viterbo University and was very committed to the local Catholic Worker community. The wife of a busy obstetrician (Paul) and mother of four children (John, Joseph, Tommy and Katie), she found time every now and then to "go on retreat" at the Benedictine monastery in Collegeville, Minnesota. She wrote to me occasionally, and kept the letters I wrote in reply. In mid-2019, Jane sent me all that trove of letters.]

Gregorian University, Rome, 22 January 1995.

[This letter refers to (a) Raymond Leo (later Cardinal) Burke, who had been ordained in Rome bishop on 6 January 1995 for the Diocese of La Crosse, and to (b) Francesco, a waiter at the Abruzzi trattoria, near the Gregorian. Jane, Bernie, and others from La Crosse dined there with me when they came for the episcopal ordination of Burke earlier in the month.]

> Dear Jane, You are an absolute treasure. You are so thoughtful towards Francesco. I will deliver your greetings and the dollars to him as soon as possible, probably this evening. I will have a friend for life there. You are simply a model of sensitivity—a lovely example for me. It was a splendid evening [at the Abruzzi], and I felt blessed again by the company of Bernie and his friends.
>
> A lovely Sunday here. In a few minutes I am off to the North American College for the twelve o'clock Mass—with Bishop Ray Burke presiding and preaching. I will stay on for lunch; it's a great chance of catching up with some of the students.
>
> Please remember our work here in your prayers. My very best to you, Bernie and the others. Peace and love for 1995, Gerald O'Collins, SJ.

Gregorian University, Rome, 21 May 1995.

> Thank you very much for the book (still to be read), the photos, and the news. I had read the *Life* article and, like you. thought the contributors or many of them a rum lot. The art was ok. At the end of June I leave Rome to lecture for a couple of days at Seton Hall University [Newark, NJ] and then for

three weeks at the University of San Francisco. At the end of July, I head on to Australia, and return to Rome in mid-September.

No, I haven't so far seen the Aids Quilt, but have been deeply saddened by the deaths of two young friends: an Australian girl and now a New York layman (young enough also). Yes, I do remember Fr Gerald Fisher [a close friend of Bernie] and was glad he put *Experiencing Jesus* [a book I published in 1994] into your hands. Please encourage him and Bernie to invest in my *Christology*, coming out right now with Oxford University Press, New York.

Your brother-in-law [a Redemptorist priest] must know loads of my Redemptorist friends here in Rome. I eat a pizza with three of them every six weeks or so. Please remember me and my students and colleagues in your prayers. A special prayer too for the real success of the summit meeting I am organizing in New York for Easter 1996.

I have to go into silence, so to speak, now (with a huge amount of examining) and then over the summer. In the meantime, peace and love to you and yours, Gerry O'C.

Gregorian University, Rome, January 1996.

[This letter refers to the wedding of Gesine Doria Pamphilj and Sylvia de Bertodano, as well as to a forthcoming conference on the resurrection at Dunwoodie and a sacred concert in St Patrick's Cathedral, New York. For details, see my *On the Left Bank of the Tiber* (Brisbane: Connor Court, 2013). *Four Weddings and a Funeral* was a popular film starring Hugh Grant.]

Dear Jane, Instead of *Four Weddings and a Funeral* [a 1994 film starring Hugh Grant], 1995 brought me two weddings that I blessed (one in the Church of Saint Agnes in the Piazza Navona and the other in the private chapel of an old Catholic home near Oxford), two weddings that I missed (those of my nephews Dominic Coleman and James Peters), a number of homecomings, and no funerals.

At Easter I went back to the ecumenical centre at Ammerdown in Somerset, to lead a group of forty people in the celebration of Holy Week and Easter. Several young people inspired us with their singing, and old Lord Hailsham supplied some mature wisdom. I hadn't visited Ammerdown since 1985. In late July, after teaching again at the University of San Francisco for three weeks of a summer school, I spent a few days in Brisbane [Australia] and gave a public lecture on Jesus' resurrection. The last time I had seen Brisbane was in 1979. A delightful surprise was the liveliness of the theology and philosophy department at the campus of Australian Catholic University. The chairperson, Pauline Allen, had just seen published the translation she and her husband did of the second part of volume two of [Cardinal Aloys] Grillmeier's *Christ in Christian Tradition*. Before returning from Melbourne to Rome, I took two weeks (from the end of August) in Perth, lecturing for the University of Notre Dame Australia in their lovely Fremantle setting. It had been four years since I had seen Perth, and it was in its spring glory. With around one thousand students and an extraordinarily dedicated staff, UND is still very much in its honeymoon days.

Like so many others in Rome, I felt very relieved that peace seems to have come at last in Bosnia. The killing and suffering have been so close, and often enough people brought us first-hand news from Sarajevo and elsewhere. In May and June I helped a little in getting three young Bosnian Muslims off to the USA.

Whatever may be happening elsewhere, the Gregorian continues to have a slight rise each year in those enrolled for theology. We have over 1,500 this current year. The quality remains high and the diversity is amazing. In my first semester course on the use of the Scriptures in systematic theology, the 290 students include, for instance, a young Lutheran bishop from Russia. The English College never fails with its Christmas pantomime. The year they did a version of *The Wizard of Oz*. After the interval, yours truly was "dragged up" onto the stage to play the Snowman.

BBC Radio Two had me doing "Pause for Thought" eight times during Lent and Easter, and six times from Advent to the Epiphany. I nurture the dream that if I soldier on with them, I might be allowed to move up to Radio Four or even the World Service. Ambition! [In fact I went on to do several interviews with Radio Four, not least for the funeral of Pope John Paul II, and many interviews on TV with the World Service.]

My very best to Bernie McGarty, your family and your excellent self. Peace and good cheer, G. O'C.

PS On Wednesday 10 April, there is a special, sacred concert [featuring Luciano Pavarotti] scheduled in St Patrick's [Cathedral, New York]. The open day at Dunwoodie is Thursday 11 April.

Gregorian University, Rome, 17 March 1996.

[This letter refers to the death of Bishop Raymond Burke's mother. The previous year Ray had become Bishop of La Crosse; after moving to be Archbishop of St Louis in 2004, he would move in 2008 to serve in the Vatican as a cardinal.]

Dear Jane, Thank you very much for your letter and the notice about the death of Ray Burke's mother. He was in Rome earlier this week, as the director of a doctoral thesis that was being defended. I saw him across the dining room at the North American College, but was not able to chat with him. I am sorry that I didn't know about his mother's death then, as I would have tried harder to get to speak with him.

In New York the sacred concert is being held on Wednesday evening (April 10) in St Patrick's Cathedral. I don't know the hour. But with the other scholars coming to the meeting, I simply will not have any time free, not even for my niece [Joanna Peters] and her family who live right there in Manhattan. Thank you for the dinner invitation, but arrangements are out of my hands and in those of the New York organizers. On Thursday 11 April, from about 9.30 to 4 o'clock at St Joseph's Seminary, Dunwoodie, Yonkers, New York, there is an open day—for teachers of religious education, clergy, and interested folk—on the resurrection. I lecture at that, and then fly out the same evening for Rome.

Apropos of all these arrangements you might give St Joseph's Seminary a phone call: (914) 968 6200. They are handling all the details. What I have done for them is provide the nineteen scholars who will meet in a closed session (Monday to Wednesday lunch time) and produce a book [on Jesus's resurrection]. I am sorry not to know more of about the details concerning the sacred concert on the Wednesday evening and the open day on the Thursday. But I have left all the practical details about the concert, the open day, etc to them. I would have been absurd on my part to try to organize the details from the banks of the Tiber.

Peace, love and a happy, grace-filled Easter, G. O'C.

Gregorian University, Rome, 11 December 1997.

[This letter refers to a Christmas break with relatives in Boscastle, Cornwall.]

Dear Jane, Thank you very much for your fascinating letter from China and now your missive about the Holy Land/Rome trip being cancelled. Too bad.

A lovely, big Christmas tree has already gone up in the Piazza Venezia [Rome], complete with a star on the top. Late Advent brings its meetings (e.g. the Gregorian University's Senate), doctoral defences, carol concerts, and goodness knows what else.

I will be relieved to board a (free) BA flight for London on 20 December, and escape to Cornwall for some days. In the meantime, every blessing for Christmas and the New Year, or, as we say in these parts, *Buon Natale e Felice Anno Nuovo.* Gerald O'Collins, SJ.

Marquette University Jesuit Residence, 14 September 1998.

[Having taught for a summer school at the University of Notre Dame, I had arrived at Marquette University as a visiting professor for a semester.]

Dear Jane, Greetings from Marquette. As you can see, I am edging my way towards La Crosse, having made it across the waters [Lake Michigan] from South Bend, Indiana. Bernie [McGarty] has me coming to preach in the parish the weekend of 14/15 November, and to sign copies of my latest book, *All Things New* (Paulist Press). Lack of modesty? Help to the publisher? Interpretations vary.

Happy days and looking forward to meeting all the available Steingraebers, as well as Bishop Ray [Burke]. Cheers, O'C.

Marquette University Jesuit Residence, 15 November 1998.

[This letter is addressed to Jane, her husband Paul, and two of their children.]

Dear Jane, Paul, Kate and Tom, Before any time elapses, I want to thank you so much for your wonderful hospitality (and apples too—they must be the best in the world). Only two more of your family to meet now, and I really look forward to welcoming John [one of them] in Rome next January. You are a lovely family, and you left me with a warm, warm glow about La Crosse.

Please tell all the other eucharistic ministers how struck I was by your dignity and gowns. There were so many things about the way you celebrate the Eucharist that I found most helpful, and not least the eucharistic ministers. I guess Collegeville

[Minnesota] extends its liturgical influence vigorously in all directions. God bless Godfrey [Diekmann, OSB] and the rest of the Benedictines.

Every blessing now for Thanksgiving and the start of Advent. And, once again, my affectionate thanks for all your hospitable kindness. May all things be truly new for you. Peace, love and good cheer, Gerry O'C. PS Kate, I hope your ankle is ok again.

Gregorian University, Rome, 18 January 1999.

My dear Jane, Today I fly off to the USA (Florida, to be precise)—only for a week—to give a retreat to the Knights and Dames of Malta. Are they in union with the other groups? What is their status? Who knows? But at least they are a devout lot, with names like Rocco Martino and Joseph Dempsey. I am back in Rome on 25 January.

These last two days I have been engaged with NBC television, the first time since about 1980, on a film about the papal succession. It goes out with Tom Brokaw [the anchor and managing editor of NBC Nightly News for twenty-two years] on 25 or 26 January at 6.30 New York time. The team includes Stefano (Italian sound-man), dark-haired Carol from London (presumably bureau chief), James (handsome reviewer), and Jim (a wonderful camera-man from Florida and a really cheerful guy like one of your boys). Over in the Vatican no one much wants to talk; so they cross the Tiber and ask over here at the Gregorian. I scored instant points with Steve Weeke, the huge leader of NBC's team: "everyone must ask you this. But are you related to Marjorie?" "My mother," he told me. The said Marjorie works for an archbishop in charge of Vatican communications, and has always been very decent to me. She certainly opened up all that she could for this NBC expedition, including filming a Mass inside St Peter's. You can read about Marjorie in John Cornwell's *Thief in the Night*. John is uncharitable to her. He tried to explain why, but I wasn't convinced.

The Vatican's Holy Office, now called the Congregation for the Doctrine of the Faith, has to read its way through 180 pages of response to their efforts to nail an old Belgian friend of mine, Jacques Dupuis, for heresy. He has just sent in his reply to their incredible accusations. Their task is now made a little harder by a wonderful article in defence of Dupuis in the latest number of the London *Tablet*. It came from the retired archbishop of Vienna, Cardinal König. Good on you, Cardinal König, I say. I had felt a little out there in front, with no one at my side, after my letter to the *Tablet* of 12 December.

Thanks for your Christmas card, letter, and son, Johnny. It was really good to meet him, even if I was a bit worn out after the NBC folk. They are perfectionists. Johnny told me of the big birthday [Jane's 50th?]. So very, very, very happy returns.

Despite all the above, life on the banks of the Tiber is quiet, normal and very academic. Peace and love to Paul, Tommy, Joseph and Johnny, not to mention the immortal Bernard and the rest, and yourself. O'C. PS I hope dear, tiny Patrick is growing away happily and healthily. [Delivered by Paul, Patrick was a very premature baby whose parents belonged to Bernard's parish in La Crosse. At less than nine months from his conception, the baby gave us all great joy when we met him one Sunday in church.]

Gregorian University, Rome, 27 June 1999

Dear Jane, Thank you very much for your April letter and all its news. My very best to John and all the family. And to Bernard. The celebration [of Jane's birthday] must have been out of this world. By the way, NBC promises to do better by me at the next conclave, whenever it comes. They want me to be their local commentator. Last Sunday I did an interview for Irish TV. But NBC at the conclave will be the real thing. But when? None of us are getting any younger. [The conclave that elected Benedict XVI came in April 2005, and I spent my time with BBC, not with NBC.]

This summer I give some lectures at a priests' institute in New Jersey, and then fly right across the country to Portland, Oregon for two days of lectures to a convention of teachers. After that, down to San Francisco (to see a niece, her family, my dear friend Dan Kendall, and some others) and then on to Australia. I return to Rome on 1 September.

Today is a lovely Sunday morning here in Rome, with a number of Romans (who are lucky enough to have a day off on Tuesday, the feast of Peter and Paul) making what they call a "bridge" for themselves—away for a long weekend from Friday until Wednesday. Is it then really worth coming back to the office on Wednesday, when next week is half way over? I have done some packing and thought I deserved a break from all that forward planning; it involves two months away from the Gregorian. And so I have switched on the good machine and can write to you.

An English friend passed on to me recently some quotes taken from medical records dictated by physicians: for instance, "the patient refused an autopsy"; "the patient has no past history of suicides"; "discharge status: alive but without permission."

Our local trattoria soldiers on. But the favourite waiter, Francesco, has retired [see letter of 22 January 1995]. Peace, love, and good cheer to you all, Gerry O'C.

PS You might tell Kate that at a birthday party right in the middle of old Rome—it was in the Doria palace actually—I met another Kate, the girlfriend of a young guy (George) whom I have known since he was a child. This Kate is English, charming, a lover of Latin, pretty, but clearly not into sport. I am absolutely in favour of her studying Latin, but she needs to remember the old principle about a healthy mind in a healthy body (*mens sana in corpore sano*). [Jane's daughter Kate excelled at sport, above all, basket ball.]

Gregorian University, Rome, 15 October 1999.

[The letter refers to Clement XIV, a Franciscan pope who suppressed the Society of Jesus in 1773.]

My dear Jane, Thank you very much for your letter which has been on my desk and conscience for some time. It's the opening of the [academic] year and that's the problem.

On Monday 11 October the Gregorian's academic year got under way again. I have more than 240 students in the first-year class on Christology. The big colleges (e.g. the North American College, Seminario Romano, and Redemptoris Mater) are well represented as usual, and there is a wide spread of others, including Oratorians (from the UK and elsewhere) whom I have never before taught.

We had the opening academic Mass on the previous Saturday, 9 October, with a big crowd filling the Basilica of the Twelve

Apostles. Normally we use San Ignazio for that opening Mass, but some repairs are taking place there—as indeed all over Rome, in preparation for the Great Jubilee [of 2,000]. The only problem with the Franciscan basilica was the public address system, which refused to work properly. Our old "enemy," Pope Clement XIV, is buried in the basilica, and I think his restless spirit was at work to mess things up every now and then.

Right now I am waiting to be hit with the proofs of a new, updated and enlarged edition of *A Concise Dictionary of Theology*, which Edward Farrugia wrote with me almost ten years ago. Paulist Press plans to put out the new, millennium edition next March. Hence I presume they will give Ed and myself very little time for correcting the proofs and adding an index to the book.

Ugh! I see that Bernard [McGarty] has probably left already for "down under." But my brother Glynn (Dr Glynn O'C) is at 69 Great Valley Road, Glen Iris, Victoria 3146. That's a suburb of Melbourne. Phone: (03) 9809 1702. His wife's name is Barbara.

My love to all, Gerry O'C.

Gregorian University, Rome, 5 January 2000.

Dear Jane, Greetings and every blessing for the new millennium. I was so pleased to hear from you and learn all the news, both agreeable and disagreeable. Altar girls! My first, wonderful contact with them was years ago (in the 1960s) on army bases in Germany. They were much more reliable than the altar boys. when I dashed around to say in several places for the US army. [Jane must have told me of someone limiting or abolishing altar girls.]

Well '99 is over. The funniest thing of the year had to be listening to Franco Zeffirelli, at a meeting on films held in the Gregorian, berating the Vatican for failing to acknowledge his contributions—through his films on Jesus, and Francis & Clare. Sitting next to Zeffirelli was Cardinal Poupard, who heard it all with an expressionless face. My major act of self-control over the last year was meeting Tolkien's daughter Priscilla, and deciding not to ask what it was like to hear the Hobbits from the horse's mouth.

Enclosed is something that tells you what I have been up to in publishing [*The Tripersonal God*, Paulist Press]. In a more popular, or rather a more spiritual, vein, I wrote *Following the Way*, a book attempting to lay out some of the major lines of Jesus' spirituality from his parables. Australian nerve! At all events HarperCollins (London) have already published it. The US publisher should be either Paulist Press or WestminsterJohn Knox. Yes, I have finished revising for Paulist Press *A Concise Dictionary of Theology*. It should be out this coming March.

Thanks for going to that trouble about forwarding the information to Bernard. It must have reached him, because my brother in Melbourne reported having Fr. B. around for a delightful evening. I spent Christmas in Cornwall with some relatives, and then went off to Somerset and a retreat center near Bath, where I led a retreat for around fifty people (mainly laypersons, including Priscilla Tolkien) that took us from 29 December to 2 January.

Peace, love and good cheer for the great jubilee to all of you, Gerald O'C.

Gregorian University, Rome, 15 March 2000.

Dear Jane and all the Steingraebers, Thank you for the wonderful photos, the cuttings, and all the news (about the good things and the things like the mammoth monstrosity that should be laid to rest). [The reference was to twenty-five million dollars that Bishop Ray Burke spent on building a shrine to the Blessed Virgin Mary. Many thought the money should have been spent on social services for the poor.]

In Rome the three days of St Patrick's Day festivities begin this evening, with a reception at the residence of the Irish Ambassador to the Holy See. I am limiting my celebration of the great saint to this evening's reception. But one could also go to the reception at the Irish Embassy to the Italian Republic, to the Masses at St Patrick's Church (off the Via Veneto) and a Mass (with shamrocks distributed afterwards, courtesy of Aer Lingus) at the nearby church of the Irish Franciscans, and to the gala, into-the-night concert at the Irish College. The College also features a Mass and a big dinner.

At Easter I will be once again in New York, co-chairing with Steve Davis (of Claremont, California) an interdisciplinary, ecumenical meeting on the incarnation, "modestly" called our Incarnation Summit. Alas, I simply fly into New York and then fly back to Rome straight after the function. You might see a little of it on TV. The first time round (Easter 1996) various networks carried something of our Resurrection Summit. NBC news was here a week ago, fascinated as so many networks and journalists were by the Pope's call to *penitence* about the bad things in the Church's past [and present]. The Mass in St Peter's last Sunday touched a lot of hardened hearts in Rome, including that of an Anglican journalist who came to Rome twenty-five years ago to work for the British papers and the

BBC. He has been here and seen it all, but the old Pope really got to David [Willey], as he did to me.

In the summer I will fly from Rome to Chicago and South Bend, to teach a three-week course (on the Trinity) at Notre Dame. But I am already angling slightly for a return to Milwaukee, in a year or so. Please pray that I pull that off. [I did return for the fall semester of 2006/2007.]

A dog, a very, very large Great Dane, keeps me healthy. I take him out for a walk from his owners' home [the Doria Palace] once or twice a week. He stops tourists, policepersons, children, and all manner of folk. He is extremely large and, most people agree, handsome.

Paulist Press will publish my *Following the Way*, a paperback on the spirituality of Jesus' parables, which HarperCollins (London) put out at the end of 1999. I am glad that HarperCollins did the right thing and made Paulist Press their US outlet; it will be my 23rd book with Paulist Press. They should make me an honorary director.

My love to all of you, and *saluti affettuosi* [affectionate best wishes] to Bernie, Gerald O'C.

Gregorian University, Rome, 10 May 2000.

Dear Jane, Thank you very much for your Easter greetings (on that wonderful card). We all need them, even more than Christmas greetings. No, the TV did not show up for the Incarnation Summit at Dunwoodie (New York). The meeting was superb, and the book, which is to come out in the middle of 2001 (with Oxford University Press, Oxford and New York), looks excellent. Do look for a special number on CNN (about seminarians and the training of priests in 2000); you will see your Gregorian connection interviewed by Hada Elena Messia, the CNN person in Rome. She said it would be shown in a "few months time."

The British Ambassador to the Holy See and his wife, Mark and Jill Pellew, just asked me to join them on Thursday. to hear Haydn's *Creation* performed by the London Philharmonic at the Vatican—for the Pope's 80th birthday. In perhaps the most notable triumph of duty over pleasure in my recent years, I had to decline. Alas that evening I will be presiding over a meeting at the Beda College. If only I was not the chairperson, I would have apologized and slipped off with the Pellews.

This summer, 8–28 July I am at the University of Notre Dame to teach in a summer school. In a day or so, I am going to write to Marquette to check whether they might like me back 2001/2002, at least in the fall of 2001. Let's see and hope. [Marquette had me back in the fall of 2006.] Happy days and much love to you and all the dear Steingraebers, Gerry O'C.

PS I hope you liked the piece in the Easter number of the London *Tablet*. Life is so full; I fondly imagine that I can stay in touch with relatives and friends by putting something into the *Tablet*.

University of Notre Dame, Indiana, 10 July 2001.

Dear Jane, Thank you for your May letter and birthday greetings. No new book to report after *Following the Way* (Paulist Press). The royalties are not that much, but they line the pockets of the Jesuit treasurer. Tomorrow is St Benedict's feast day, a good time to write to someone who rightly prizes the O.S.Bs.

I resonate with (a) your feeling at your best when praying in church with everyone, and (b) with the feeling that compulsory celibacy is hard to understand.

Lots of girls (and boys) in Italy, the USA, etc are a bit insecure and "fragile," I think to myself. Instinct leads me to try to be the best of friends to them. I felt that Katie was a little that way, and I cherish her for it. So please give her my VERY best. One day I will tell you about Sylvia, an English girl who is a bit like that. I did her wedding a few years ago; she and her lovely husband Stuart work as lawyers in the war crime trials around the world. Katie is a darling, but I don't want her to work in international courts. It's tough life. [In the letter of January 1996, I refer to Sylvia's wedding.]

I hope South Africa treats you very well. My love to all the Steingraebers. *Pace e bene* [peace and everything good], G. O'C.

Gregorian University, Rome, 31 January 2000.

My dear Jane, Thanks for all the news, especially of the family. I was glad that you liked my piece in the Christmas number of *America* magazine. The teaching work at Viterbo College sounds wonderful.

January ends today, and it has been a very full month. In fact, it started in December, when I went over to Washington to lecture and preach at St Patrick's in the City. The last day, Epiphany Sunday, was , made memorable by a mega-Mass for the John Carroll Society: chief celebrant Uncle Avery (alias Cardinal) Dulles, and preacher your truly. Over brunch the JC Society awarded John Carroll Society Medals to Avery and myself—a lovely gesture which I hadn't expected.

I was hardly back in Rome before I flew off to preach in Belfast and Armagh during the week of prayer for Christian Unity. My Anglican, Catholic, and Presbyterian hosts were a delight. But I wondered and worried about others, like the small group of demonstrators outside St Anne's Cathedral (Church of Ireland) who held up placards ("What has Christ to do with Belial?") and who harassed a delightful Salvation Army couple when they arrived for the service. I felt like calling out: "Please leave the Salvos alone!"

The night before I arrived, almost the whole population of Northern Ireland seemed to have watched on TV "Bloody Sunday." Someone had taped it, and later I was able to see part of it. The portrayal by James Nesbitt of Ivan Cooper [the civil rights leader who co-founded the Social-Democratic and Labour Party, SDLP, and on 30 January 1972 led an anti-internment march that was fired on by British troops] was gripping. The most astonishing thing for me, on this my first visit to Northern Ireland since 1965, was the total invisibility of the security forces. Apart from one or two police I saw at the airport, I never caught sight of any police in Belfast, Armagh, or along the roads. The only soldier, if you can call him that, whom I met or even saw was the Anglican chaplain to the troops hidden away in the barracks at Armagh. Patrick had studied at my Cambridge College (Pembroke College), and so we had a lot of friends to talk about.

It would be a delight if Joseph turns up in Rome. Apart from 2–11 April (in New York to give two lectures), I am at the Gregorian until the end of June. Then I teach for three weeks at the University of Notre Dame [Indiana], before flying on to my niece [Marion Peters] in San Francisco, to Australia, and back to Rome at the very start of September. No Marquette, as you can see. But I did write to them yesterday, [and asked] in the spirit of "Barkis is willing," if they have something in mind for me.

Peace and love to all of you, Gerald O'C. PS I would like to read that piece on Judi Dench. a fantastic actress. Did you ever see her in *Tea With Mussolini*?

Gregorian University, Rome, 1 May 2002.

Dear Jane, Thanks for the material on the passing to the Lord of dear, wonderful Godfrey Diekmann. I was so pleased at the news about Tommy [engagement?]. Your idea of flopping on the beach (preferably on an island in the Pacific) with a gin and tonic also crosses my mind at times.

Yes, there is "nothing better than being loved." I would only add—"being loved with a bit of humour." Little Eduardo, the grandson of an old friend of mine and a four-year-old who looks like an extraordinary male version of Shirley Temple, rushed up to me recently, gave me a huge hug. and then stepped back to poke me in the stomach and say, "Pancia." That's a very economic expression for "you are putting on weight." The Italians have a bad name for using many words, but sometimes they can say things extremely briefly and humorously.

It would be great to see Joseph if he changes his plans [and visits Rome]. Congratulations on your zestful and obviously successful teaching [of nursing]. Thanks too for the news about Kate. Please give her my love and ask her to put nutmeg on the cappuccino. Bernie [Monsignor McGarty] turned up recently out of the blue. But, alas, I had another appointment that evening (with a great group of Asian students) and could not take up his invitation to supper. Peace, love and good cheer to all the family, Gerald.

Gregorian University, Rome, 16 January 2003.

[For many years Jane and her friend Barb Kruse led the local CROP Hunger Walk, an international initiative sponsored by Church Walk Service and organized by religious groups, businesses, schools, and others aimed at raising funds to end world hunger. In La Crosse many Catholics walked and contributed. A certain Arthur Hippler, on the staff—apparently in a social justice capacity— for Bishop Burke, came up with a false story that, along with the food being sent to South America, contraceptives were also included in the shipments. The regional director of CROP tried to correct the misinformation but to no avail. The local Catholic high school, at one time the biggest fundraiser, dropped out. Bishop Burke sent to all the parishes a letter forbidding promotion of CROP. The prohibition, based on false information, did great damage.]

Dear Jane, A very blessed New Year to you and all the family and thanks for the news, even if what Arthur Hippler & Co have been doing makes me very sad. Please keep up the struggle for truth, justice and transparency. If you want a comment or two from a moral theologian, why not try Fr John Paris, SJ, who I think is still at Boston College? He is outstanding; if you contact him, please tell him that I suggested it.

Looking back with thanks at the year which has just closed down, I feel very grateful at the chance of revisiting New Zealand and Oxford. In August I was back for a week in Christchurch and Auckland, to give several lectures to lay people and priests. It was a lovely reminder of how beautiful that country is and how outgoing and truly democratic the Kiwis are. From mid-October, I spent five weeks in Oxford, to give the Martin D'Arcy lectures sponsored by Campion Hall. Faith in the resurrection was my theme, and Darton, Longman and Todd (and Paulist Press) will publish the book around September 2003.

Those weeks in Oxford let me catch up with such old friends as Henry Chadwick and John Macquarrie. The cheerful courage with which they and others face old age and health problems was astonishingly edifying and made me pray to share in such a grace.

On the publishing front, I finally saw through to publication (May 2002) *The Incarnation* (Oxford University Press), which I co-edited with Steve Davis and Dan Kendall. There were all kinds of difficulties along the way including a corrupt font which also did its bit in setting back the date of the book's appearance. To make up for that struggle, my own (much shorter book), *Incarnation* (Continuum) breezed through to appearance within a few months—the fastest time to publication I have ever enjoyed. Around September 2003, OUP will put out my *Catholicism*, a book they asked me to write and one that is and, no doubt, will be the longest work I have ever written. OUP have agreed to bring the book out simultaneously as a paperback and hardback. Hooray, as that can be a boon for students.

This coming Easter I am going back to Dunwoodie, for the fourth and last "summit," this time on redemption—pretty timely, I think. Most of the old gang will be there, but there will be some shining, new faces like Caroline Walker Bynum

(Columbia University). Thanks for your prayers and for your example. I know only two other Janes in the world: a cousin of mine with the BBC in London and Jane Jeffes, a wonderful English lady with the media in Australia. The three of you all set me an inspiring example. Peace, love and good cheer for 2003, Gerry.

Gregorian University, Rome, 1 March 2003.

Dear Jane, Yes, it would be lovely to see Tommy in Rome in late May. Yes, John Macquarrie did write a touching book on Mary. Alas, I have not (yet) read Jon Hassler.

Yes, I was very sorry about the sex abuse cases in the monastic community [at Collegeville, Minnesota], but better to be open. *America* magazine did very well and helpfully on the whole issue. I am proud of them, and happy every now and then (e.g. this coming Easter) to write something for [Tom] Reese [the editor]. Wonderful news about John and Shelley [engagement].

I am sorry this is all I can manage [a postcard]. But much peace and love to you all, Gerald.

Gregorian University, Rome, 20 March 2003.

Dear Jane, Thank you very much indeed for the two novels by Jon Hassler. I look forward greatly to reading them. I love the idea of foot-washing at the wedding of John and Shelley. God love them. Tommy shouldn't worry too much about a curfew in the convent selected by his uncle [a Redemptorist priest]. He (Tommy) should be able to talk the nuns into giving him a key. Let's see. Peace and love, Gerald O'C [another postcard].

Gregorian University, Rome, 6 June 2003.

Dear Jane, my affectionate congratulations to Kate on her graduation. Hooray! I was really sorry to miss Tom on his visit to Rome. The day he phoned I was down at Salerno giving two lectures [at the seminary]. Hopefully his uncle looked after him really well.

We are in the midst of exams. I leave for the summer on 15 July and return to my Roman base on 22 September. Peace, love, and good cheer, Gerald O'C [another postcard].

Gregorian University, Rome, 3 July 2003.

Dear Jane, Last Monday I returned from lecturing to the priests of Down and Conner (or is it Down and Connor?) diocese in Northern Ireland, where the situation remains a kind of cold peace. But it certainly is a big change. after three decades of civil war. One of the priests told me about cradling in his arms a nineteen-year-old British soldier who died after being shot by a sniper. Another priest had his two parish houses firebombed and lost, among other things, his library which contained one or two books by yours truly. That same priest, in another parish, found his Doberman a bit restive around six one evening. He opened the door and she bolted around the corner to surprise three men about to firebomb the church. Two of them ran for their lives; the other was a bit slow and the Doberman sank her teeth into his leg. The police picked him up later in the casualty section of a nearby hospital—the only patient to be admitted that evening with a wound caused by a dog.

This evening, the eve of Independence Day. I go to a reception staged by the US Ambassador to the Holy See. We are to be entertained by a country and western band and, outside, by a couple of cowboys. On the 5th I go out of Rome to make my annual retreat in a house up in the [Alban] hills. After that I leave for England and the USA on the 15th.

I arrive on Tuesday 5 August in Sydney to stay at St Aloysius College on the harbour. On Thursday 7th in the crypt of St Patrick's Church Hill, I am giving a lecture (6–8 pm) on Easter faith. The evening has been arranged by Catalyst for Renewal. Hopefully the resurrection can renew all of us. Then on Friday 8th I leave for Melbourne in the morning. Eventually back to Rome on 22 September, after some lecturing in Perth, one of the loveliest cities I know. No pollution, beautiful wild flowers in the spring etc.

I hope Kate has a marvellous start at Loyola [University, Chicago?]. My love to her, you. and all the family, Gerald O'C.

Gregorian University, Rome, 5 October 2003.

My dear Jane, This has been my Anglican week, teaching a course on Jesus—who else is really worth talking about?— for a group of Anglican clergy and laity, and sharing in the sacred and secular celebrations of the first visit to Rome of Rowan Williams, the new Archbishop of Canterbury. On Friday afternoon I did an interview with the BBC on the visit, trying to cope with questions like: is there a difference between difficulties created by the Anglicans ordaining women and ordaining gays? On Saturday (at 4 pm) hundreds of locals and visitors filled the Basilica of Santa Maria sopra Minerva for a prayer service, featuring not only Williams himself but also

Cardinal Walter Kasper (the head of the Pope's Council for Christian Unity) and Cardinal Cormac Murphy-O'Connor of London.

After praying and singing together, we sloped off to the private apartments of the young Prince Doria Pamphilj—his palace is very close—to a reception. There were several hundred visitors from the UK, and I wandered around shaking hands and sharing a bit of local knowledge with them. A smaller group went off after the reception to the home of the British Ambassador to the Holy See, for a dinner in honour of Rowan Williams and his wife Jane. The five tables for the guests were named after cathedrals in England. I was on the Winchester table.

I was very sorry to hear that Katie and Paul had been laid low. I have said a Mass for them and all the Steingraebers. Yes, I do know Fr Garanzini [then President of Loyola University, Chicago?], but haven't seen much of him since he taught at the Gregorian as a visiting professor in the late 80s.

I have finally started reading *Staggerford*. Hassler is an excellent novelist. So thanks again for those two books. This coming week I fly over to Croazia to give a couple of lectures in Split. Then a week, with visitors and BBC television, covering the party for the Pope's 25th and the beatification of Mother Teresa. It has been so busy here that I am looking forward greatly to spending 22 October–30 November at the University of San Francisco, to give a handful of lectures only. Hooray! On 1 December I will be back at my Rome base. Peace and love to you all, Gerald.

Gregorian University, Rome, December 2003.

Dear Jane, Paul, John, Shelley, Joseph, Tom and Katie, Every blessing at Christmas and for the New Year. I am glad you had a GREAT Oktoberfest. Congratulations, Jane, on your being Mrs Oktoberfest. 26 parades are a lot. Peace, love and good cheer, Gerry O'C [another postcard].

Gregorian University, Rome, 29 February 2004.

Dear Jane, Let me take advantage of a leap-year and write to you on 29 February. It makes me wonder again what folks do who are born today. Do they or their parents register their birthdays on 28 February or on 1 March? I still have not met someone who was born on 29 February and forced his parents to face this issue.

These days it has been snowing just to the north and east of Rome, and in other parts of Italy. What with the rain and snow, the Tiber is running high and looks a decent river for a change. This morning I went up on the roof of the Gregorian to have a look at Mount Soratte, well north of the city. Hooray, it was visible and had a nice circle of snow on its peak. I had old Horace in mind; in one of his lyrics he mentions looking north from Rome and seeing snow on that mountain.

Lord George Carey and his wife Eileen have settled into their cottage in the grounds of the Irish College, while George does six weeks of teaching at the Gregorian. They came for lunch last Thursday, and I broke Eileen's resolution to abstain from wine during Lent. That's what Jesuits do for/to you.

At Easter (probably Easter Sunday itself) I imagine that I

will be called to christen Gesine Doria's fourth child. She and Massimiliano now have four daughters: Anna, Elisa, Irene, and Orietta. After A, E, I, and O, will they have another daughter and call her by a name beginning with U? That's hard in Italian. You might use Umberta, Ugolina, or Ubalda. An emergency solution would be Ursula, normally spelt Orsola in Italian. But you can get by with names spelt in foreign style: e.g. Ivan (instead of Giovanni) and Lucy (instead of Lucia) turn up sometimes.

New Zealand is wonderfully beautiful, even if I might have died there back in 1975, when a priest pilot tried to fly me over the Southern Alps in a gale-force wind.

Loads of visitors in Rome these days: from England, Finland, Australia, and the States. My award for the jolliest visitor must go to 80-year-old Dr John Harvey from Washington, DC. He is full of pep and with a mind full of information and questions. John turns up for a week, in mid-March. Happy Lent and Easter. Peace and love to all of you, Gerald.

Gregorian University, Rome, 1 April 2004.

My dear Jane, Thanks for the letter and the wonderful photograph. What better thing to do on April 1st than write a few letters—to you and others? I am around for Easter Sunday, leaving Rome only for a few days of chat with folk at Oxford University Press and with the former editor of the London *Tablet* John Wilkins (13–18 April). British Airways has given me a free flight to London for the occasion. Apropos of first-class flights, I once was upgraded by Air France to *premier classe*. But your ride sounds better.

The University of San Francisco was a delight, and made even better by the presence of my niece (a medical professor) and her family. Back in Italy, visitors drop out of the Roman sky constantly. Last week began with forty Finns, Lutheran pastors and their spouses, who wanted to be filled in about matters Catholic and Lutheran. Then there was an American couple whose wedding I did 33 years ago; they are still very cheerfully together and are grandparents several times. Australian bishops on their ad limina visit swarmed around Rome and on 24 March I joined them at a Mass in St John Lateran's basilica, which was followed by a reception in the Irish College. A great benefactor [Dr Eugene McCarthy] was in town from New York; he has funded two [visiting] chairs at the Gregorian and flies over for the major lectures of the current chair-holders. George Carey, the former Archbishop of Canterbury, was occupying our chair in theology, giving an optional course on ecumenical affairs. But in his major, public lecture George spoke on Islam and Christianity, and, thanks to a reporter from the [London] *Telegraph*, stirred things up in the news circles of London and made some of the media outlets elsewhere.

For some peculiar reason God keeps me in good health. Does the Trinity require more books from me. Right now I am towards the end of writing a work (with John Wilkins), *Living Vatican II* [Paulist Press, 2006]. By the way, my chapter on the liturgy denounces bad preaching. After that? Yes, there are other items coming or at least planned. The Vatican II book will be published by Paulist Press as part of a series they have organized to coincide with forty years since the Council's closure.

I am in Rome till 29 June; then to Seton Hall in New Jersey

(for a week of lecturing); and reach Melbourne on 15 July. Easter peace and love to you and all the family, Gerald O'C.

Gregorian University, Rome, Easter Sunday April 2004.

Dear Jane, Of course, Tommy's friend is very welcome to phone me etc, if she needs advice or whatever when she comes in May. My phone number is (06) 6701 5360. So please tell her that, and tell her parents that.

I pray for your brother. Did I ever tell you that my medical niece (now in San Francisco) runs a liver unit? She does not do the surgery, but all the rest.

Mel Gibson's film [*The Passion of Christ*] opened last Wednesday in 26 cinemas around Rome! With their fears about terrorist attacks, the Italian security forces are also keeping an eye on those cinemas. But the young are here in Rome—en masse. I expect there will be over 100,000 at St Peter's later this morning. I am writing at 8.30 am. Peace, love and Easter good cheer, Gerald O'C.

Gregorian University, Rome, 6 February 2005.

My dear Jane, Thanks for all the news, about the wedding of Joseph and Katie Jordan. Please give them my very, very best. You recall January 1995 and Francesco at the Abruzzi restaurant [see letter of 22 January 1995]. He has retired some time ago. Singapore? I always find the Catholics and other folk there very exhilarating. They worked me hard last September (on the resurrection, Christ and the non-Christian religions, redemption etc.), but it was thoroughly worth the effort.

My book on Vatican II won't be out for a while. I finished my chapters, but the co-author, John Wilkins, is grinding his out very slowly. He was editor of the London *Tablet* for over twenty years.

No, I don't know anything about your new bishop, and do hope he proves a winner for you. Our bishop [John Paul II] got close to death last Tuesday night, but seems to be on the mend. The media poured into Rome on Wednesday, and I did a raft of interviews for the BBC, CBS, Australian and Canadian television etc, and finished off today by taking part (by phone) in a Sunday talk show in Ireland. Thousands of Irish are in Rome, by the way, to see their rugby team play Italy. The Irish should walk it in, but you never know in rugby.

Christmas was pretty overshadowed by Jacques Dupuis and his death. I buried him on 30 December in the Jesuit mausoleum in the classic, old cemetery near our main railway station. Enclosed is my obituary of Dupuis [for the London *Tablet*]. I miss the old guy, since we spent so much time together over the last eight or nine years.

On 2 January I left for London and Washington (to speak to the priests of the archdiocese and also to give (twice) a lecture on *The Da Vinci Code*). If you can lay your hands on the latest number of *Origins*, you will find an abbreviated version of that lecture. I must say, the interest is great: over 400 at each lecture.

Now, there are some noises from Marquette University about my returning for the fall semester of 2006. So let's hope and pray for that. No, I don't ski. My nephews and nieces all do, and a number of them gathered in Denver after Christmas to ski together. Much love to you all, Gerald.

Gregorian University, Rome, 19 March 2006.

My dear Jane, I was so glad you had a great trip to China, and thanks for the postcard from there (plus the one from Collegeville). A couple of Sundays back Michael Naughton, the prior of San Anselmo here in Rome, asked me to lead a day of retreat. It was good to see him again, and find him doing something new after those years at the head of Liturgical Press. You must have met him, or at least seen him [at Collegeville].

An old mate from Boston, RD Sahl, will be in Rome this week, making another film for PBS. He will interview me on Tuesday—about the new papacy. RD is a lovely person, one of the nicest I know in the media.

I will see a whole lot more of the media folk when Cardinal Pell (the Archbishop of Sydney) is in Rome on Palm Sunday to take over the World Youth Day officially (for August 2008). The Australian embassy has been busy planning a function at 5 pm on the terrace of a hotel up near the Vatican. The Cardinal's offensive against the primacy of conscience is a bit of a contradiction in terms; he has carried it on, because his conscience prods him into doing so!

I will be back at Marquette University mid-August until mid-December. Hooray! Have a wonderful Easter. Peace and love, Gerald.

Marquette University, Milwaukee, 12 September 2006.

Dear Jane, Well, I left Rome for good on 21 June, spent a few days in London (to give two lectures), then flew on to Melbourne, and—finally— got myself to Marquette at the end of August. I have a couple of classes a week (for graduates in theology) and some other duties for the theology department. It's good to be back at Marquette, where I know a good number of the Jesuits and theology faculty.

Next month my grandniece comes up from the University of Chicago, where she is a sophomore, to visit me. Abigail is great fun, and was with me in Rome several times. Any chance of your making it to Milwaukee? It would be lovely to see you again, and the "kids" also.

In mid-December I fly over to London, where the University of Surrey wants me for two years (until December 2008) as a research professor. It means living in a Jesuit community in Wimbledon, about twenty minutes by train from the campus where the theology department is. Peace, love, and good cheer, Gerald O'C.

Marquette University, Milwaukee, November 2006.

[This letter refers to the keys for a guest room in the Jesuit residence at Marquette University. Jane had stayed there, forgot to return the keys, but sent them back from La Crosse.]

Dear Jane, Thanks for the keys and your splendid e-mail. Every blessing to you and all your dear ones at Christmas and for the New Year. Please excuse this wretched letter. Let me sketch my situation. I have left, yes, left for good, the Gregorian, and from mid-December will be living in a Jesuit community in Wimbledon for two years (Dec. 2006–Dec. 2008): John Sinnott House, 8 Edge Hill, Wimbledon, London SW19 4LR, England. The phone number: 0044 20 8947 4251; fax 0044 20 8944 6571. My e-mail remains the same.

After consultation with the Australian Jesuit provincial and the British provincial, I accepted an offer from St Mary's College, Strawberry Hill (University of Surrey) to be a research professor with them for two years (Dec. 2006–Dec. 2008). The campus of St Mary's is about twenty minutes by train from Wimbledon. Right now I am finishing a semester as visiting professor at Marquette University and fly to London on 14 December.

You are an amazing example to me, even motherly love incarnate. Benedict XVI was wrong. A mother's love is THE paradigm. [In his first encyclical *Deus Caritas est*, the Pope proposed that the paradigm of love is that between spouses.]

Paulist Press will publish shortly the US edition of *The Lord's Prayer*. At the AAR meeting in Washington, I had a good chat with the charming folk from Liturgical Press [Collegeville, Minnesota]. Peace and love to you and all your dear ones, Gerry.

John Sinnott House, Wimbledon, 29 January 2007.

My dear Jane, Many thanks for the Christmas card, the e-mail, and the photos. One of the eight other Jesuits with whom I live cooked a fantastic Christmas dinner; so when I went up the hill in the evening to the home of a cousin and her husband, I could not do any justice to what they put before me.

I have been reconnecting with a range of friends. Take last week. On Monday evening I joined Bishop Tom Wright for a meal at the Athenaeum, traditionally a club which Anglican bishops join. Tom comes down from Durham for three days once a month to sit in the House of Lords. I got to know him well when he made two visits to New York for the "summit" meetings that I co-chaired. He joined us at Easter 2000 (on the incarnation) and at Easter 2003 (on the redemption). Then on Tuesday evening I walked up the hill and along the ridge beyond my cousin's home to have a meal with Geoff and Sue Chapman. He was at high school with me, and came to London to found "Geoffrey Chapman," long ago engulfed by another company but in its day a highly successful publishing firm. He sold, for instance, a million or more copies of the translation of the documents of Vatican II that Walter Abbott, SJ, edited. To round off the week, on Saturday I went up the hill again to "The Swan" for a pub lunch with a friend from Cambridge, Canon Richard Incledon. He served for many years as the Catholic chaplain at Cambridge University, succeeding Monsignor Alfred Gilbey (of the family that produced Gilbey's gin). I arrived in Cambridge for Gilbey's last term; he spent thirty-three years and one term there (one hundred terms). The trustees kept Gilbey on for one last term, so that he could reach the century.

Half way through last week there was a decent snowfall overnight. Next morning the schoolboys were pelting each other with snowballs as they went up the hill to Wimbledon College, a Jesuit high school with around 1,300 students. Wimbledon is loaded with schools, and every morning and afternoon hundreds of boys and a few girls pass my window. I am up on the second floor and enjoy a large window looking out on the street. A big girls' high school (started by the Ursulines) is a few blocks away, but not on Edge Hill.

The very old road that runs along the top of the hill is called Ridgeway (what else would you expect?). Country people would bring their sheep and other animals along that road, and could make a last stop on Wimbledon Common before heading into London to sell their beasts. Their route took them past the present site of Wimbledon tennis courts, where two thousand years ago Julius Caesar pitched camp on his famous expedition to Britain. The Romans brought along some wine, and that was supposed to be the first time the Brits ever tasted it. A local history of Wimbledon has the splendid title of *From Caesar's Camp to Centre Court.*

Peace and love to you and all the family, Gerry.

John Sinnott House, Wimbledon, 17 June 2007.

Dear Jane, Thanks for your letter and all the news—a kind of end of the academic year round up. I am just back from lunch in a pub near Wimbledon railway station with Desmond Avery, recently retired from the World Health Organization and soon to publish a book on Simone Weil (d. 1943), a remarkable French thinker treasured by Albert Camus and T. S. Eliot. I have known Desmond for a number of years, but had no idea how radical he was. I thought, wrongly, that all those years with WHO would have tamed him. No way! His book interprets and applies Weil with fierce honesty and creative fidelity to our present global situation.

Before I leave London on 27 June for a Seton Hall institute on the New Jersey shore and then two weeks for the Boston College summer school, I have a couple of days with priests in here in London—on preaching the Gospel. Maybe I will shift a few of them from the kind of moralizing summed up by an Australian poet: "Be good, be kind, and God save the Queen." So life is as full as ever.

Desmond, by the way, loves St Benedict and his rule. His favourite community of Benedictines, Pluscarden Abbey, is right up at the top of Scotland, the most northern community of Benedictines anywhere in the world. He does go there, and may join me in October 2008 when I lecture to the monks on Christ. (What other topic is worth while?)

Desmond's only child, a daughter now married in Vienna, played the violin at a wedding I celebrated some years ago outside Oxford, in the medieval home of some Catholics, descendants of St Thomas More who never accepted Henry VIII's reformation. She had hoped to be able to join the Vienna Philharmonic. The last time I saw the orchestra (on TV, New Year's Day) there was, as far as I could see, only one woman in their ranks.

A week ago I was down in Wells (Somerset) to give a lecture to a lively parish group. I had forgotten how very beautiful the medieval cathedral is. My hosts, Roger and Chris Bird, live in a house that used to be part of a vast mental hospital built in the nineteenth century along the lines of an Elizabethan farm establishment. The hospital closed in 1990, and the whole centre has been turned into homes.

After Boston, I fly out to San Francisco on 20 July and then to Australia, returning to Wimbledon on 15 September. Thanks for all your prayers and friendship. Peace and good cheer, Gerry.

John Sinnott House, Wimbledon, 3 December 2007.

My dear Jane and all your dear family, I hope you all have a wonderful Christmas together, with lots of bright snow around. We just might have some this year in the UK.

Life at St Mary's University College (Strawberry Hill, Twickenham) goes along cheerfully. They have given me a chair as research professor, an office, and various kinds of secretarial help, but ask very little in return—more or less, only that I get on with writing and publishing and mention their name whenever I give lectures in various parts of the UK and elsewhere. In early 2008, I have an academic book coming out with OUP, *Salvation for All; God's Other Peoples*, and a book on Christ for a general readership, *Jesus: A Portrait* (Darton, Longman & Todd, London; Orbis Books in the USA). That Jesus book will be my fiftieth published book. No, I didn't plan on that, but am glad that the Master himself is the theme of my 50th. I hope he likes it; otherwise I am in big trouble.

You must have read about the publication of documents concerned with the Knights Templar (suppressed in the early 14th century). The documents show that papal officials acquitted them of charges (of heresy, sodomy, and blasphemy) that had been brought against them. (If you were going to bring charges, why not throw in the lot?) The acquittal didn't stop the wicked French king (Philip) from pressuring a weak pope into suppressing the military order, so that Philip could do some looting of the Templars' property. On 25 October, the day the Vatican published facsimiles of the documents and put them on sale, BBC World Television was trying to find me for an interview. But I was away leading a group of Anglican bishops and their spouses in study and prayer. Some folk reacted to the news by asking for an apology from the Vatican. But where do you find any Templars nowadays to receive the apology? Maybe the French government should be the first to apologize and even restore some of the stolen property?

I am just back from Ammerdown Centre in Somerset, where I led an individually guided retreat for eleven people. They included a couple of Anglican women who had been ordained priests. The centre is built out of the old stables of a stately home, and one of the young members of the Jolliffe family lives in the big house with his wife and five little daughters. Andrew and Diana are very good friends and I love watching their children grow up. On this visit, coming back around 9.30 pm from the chapel (beautifully constructed out of an ancient meat store), I ran into the little girls wearing war paint. "We're on mission," they assured me, and darted away into the dark. Much love to you all for Christmas and the New Year, Gerry.

Jesuit Theological College, Parkville, 13 September 2010.

[This letter refers to Joseph W. Tobin, a Redemptorist who had been the superior general of his institute and had just been appointed to the Vatican's Congregation for Institutes of Consecrated Life and Societies of Apostolic Life. He became Archbishop of Newark and a cardinal under Pope Francis. Bishop Kevin Dowling, another Redemptorist, was bishop of Rustenberg in South Africa and an outstanding, prophetic voice.]

My dear Jane, Greetings from Melbourne, where we are gently leaving winter behind and entering spring. I do hope and pray that Joe Tobin (yes, a friend of one of my Redemptorist friends in Rome) will keep going along the good lines of his life so far and will not be corrupted. Yes, Bishop Dowling is wonderful. They spoke so well of him in South Africa, where I was lecturing mid-July to mid-August.

Yesterday, I celebrated Mass in the Newman College chapel (University of Melbourne) for the knights and dames of Malta. The gospel was that of the prodigal son. The homily needed some crafting, as I don't think there are too many prodigal sons and prodigal daughters among the knights and dames.

This coming Wednesday takes me north to Sydney to do an e-conference on "Jesus the Christ." With colleges, parishes etc. signed up, the organizers expect 50,000 or more to share in the conference, with their questions, experiences etc. This will be the fourth in a series over the last couple of years. Paul, the Blessed Virgin Mary, and St Luke have been the themes of the previous three e-conferences.

A local Melbourne daily, *The Age*, is sending a reporter to Birmingham for the beatification of John Henry Newman. It surprised me—pleasantly surprised me—that a left-leaning newspaper would be interested enough to do that. Anyway long live Newman! *The Age* is interested in the canonization of the first Australian saint, Mary MacKillop, but not to the extent of sending a reporter to Rome for the event in mid-October.

Newspapers continue to surprise me, not least *The Guardian* (UK). They have picked up quite a lot (with a review and then an interview) on my *Philip Pullman's Jesus* that Darton, Longman & Todd have just published. A few months ago Pullman published his *The Good Man Jesus and the Scoundrel Christ*, and

DLT asked me to write at high speed a response—a task that was made easier by the reviews of Pullman's book and interviews with him. In the UK, his book was still the talk of the town last Easter and triggered at least thirty worthwhile reviews and interviews. Peace, love and good cheer in the Lord, Gerald.

Jesuit Theological College, Parkville, 5 August 2012.

Dear Jane, That was wonderful news about Katie's PhD. Please give her my warmest congratulations. Thanks for all the other news as well.

Last month the London *Tablet* carried an article by me ("The Art of the Possible") on the highly necessary reform of the Congregation for the Doctrine of the Faith (July 14). As the CDF has just changed its leader ("prefect"), there was a chance of saying something, in the vague hope that one might be listened to.

The editor of *America* plans a special number in October to mark fifty years since the Second Vatican Council opened and asked a number of people to say (in 800 words) where they found the Council's greatest impact today. So I have written something on the Council's commitment to peace and justice, along with a grateful reference to Dorothy Day and her associates. The editor of the *Tablet* has also planned a special number for next October, and asked for a longer piece. So I wrote something along the lines of reform in relations with "others" scoring good marks, whereas reform within the Church needing a lot more implementation (e.g. the failure to put through real collegiality and, now the reform of the reform of the liturgy with the clunky words and latinized English that have been imposed on us).

In October I will fly to London and, for the diocese of Plymouth, give some lectures (on Vatican II, of course) for lay people and clergy in Winchester. At the end of the two weeks, I will have a few days free in London before heading home to Melbourne.

Last month volume one of my autobiography came out, and the publisher kept me busy by laying on three launches (two in Melbourne and one in Sydney). Later this month he has another launch in Canberra (carrying the good news to the capitol city?). Enclosed is the flyer he used for the first launch. Peace, love, and good cheer, Gerry.

Jesuit Theological College, Parkville, 18 August 2013.

My dear Jane, Thanks for your letter of 18 July and all the news. Yes, Jacques Dupuis was the priest for whom I spoke before the CDF. Last year Bill Burrows published a couple of articles by Dupuis, and the book received a rather snooty review in the London *Tablet* for 22 June 2013. (I wrote a letter of protest for the issue of July 7, 2013, protest not against the editor but against the reviewer, Gavin D'Costa.) Yes, Ratzinger never read the 180-page answer Dupuis put together in response to the first blast he received from the CDF in 1998. The cardinal said just that at the September 2000 hearing [attended by myself as adviser to Dupuis].

I rejoice in the way St John's Abbey [Collegeville] is a spiritual home for you. God love the Benedictines.

These days I have been doing some writing etc. for a committee formed to raise money to restore a proper study of Latin and Greek at the University of Melbourne. The University let Latin and Greek run down badly, and a number of us who treasured our studies in the classics are trying to reverse the trend. Without the classics, the history of the Jesuits would be unthinkable. Mary Beard, professor of classics at the University of Cambridge, wrote a great piece, "Do the Classics have a Future?," in the *New York Review of Books* for 12 January 2012.

35 extra students in your class sounds a lot more, as it takes you to a class of 133!!! A class merely of 35 would be big enough anyway.

I have four launches of my *On the Left Bank of the Tiber* (= Rome from 1974 to 2006). The *National Catholic Reporter* plans to run some extracts from the chapter on the Dupuis affair. Over the years I have done only one launch of any book I've written. [In fact, two: one in Boston in 1969 (very successful) and one in London in 2002 (a disaster).] But the local, Australian publisher believes in launches and his efforts make them reasonable successes. Paulist Press will publish the book in the US. [In fact, they did not.]

This afternoon I will have coffee with Steve Evans, a lovely scholar and human being from Baylor University (Texas). A world expert on Kierkegaard, Steve is in Melbourne for a conference celebrating two hundred years since the birth of K.

Every blessing to you and all your dear ones. Peace, love, and good cheer, Gerry O'C.

Part VI:
Christmas Letters
(2009 to 2019)

Christmas 2009

"With joy you will draw water from the wells of salvation"—psalm for the Third Sunday of Advent.

The BIG event of 2009 was relocating my base of operations from Wimbledon to the Jesuit Theological College in the Melbourne suburb of Parkville. The college, which consists of ten terrace houses built in the late nineteenth century, faces Royal Parade, a spacious avenue decorated with lines of elms and heading towards Sydney. My office, on the first floor, looks through the trees at the traffic and beyond, to the tennis courts of University College. My bedroom at the back (also on the first floor) looks out to the West and the playing fields and trees of Royal Park. Birds galore hang around in the trees and shrubs out the back: magpies, doves, wattle birds, mudlarks, butcher birds, parrots of various persuasions, willy wagtails (fantail flycatchers), Australian mynahs, and some assorted imports like blackbirds, Indian mynahs, pigeons, and the occasional sparrow.

In August/September I left London with a bang: two weddings and a funeral, not to mention the Tablet Lecture and the lovely dinner that Catherine Pepinster hosted when the captains, kings, and princesses had departed after my Tablet Lecture (followed by a reception) in Heythrop College.

Writing continues: next March Oxford University Press will publish *Jesus Our Priest*, an ecumenical study of the priesthood of Christ, co-authored with Michael Keenan Jones. Trips will continue: the first will involve chairing a meeting (of theologians and scientists) for the Templeton Foundation in Oxford (at the Randolph Hotel) April 15-17. The theme is 'Light from Light', and Eerdmans (Grand Rapids, Michigan) seem interested in publishing the proceedings. [They did.]

A very happy and blessed Christmas and New Year to you and all your dear ones.

Christmas 2010

As 2010 moves towards its close, the year sorts itself out and the landmark events of 2010 become clearer. For myself and my family, the death of Jim Peters at the age of 96 marked the year. A handsome medical doctor, just discharged from the army, he married my eldest sister Moira in early 1946. As a teenage boy at the wedding reception I was given the task of chatting with an elderly lady festooned with pearls and diamonds. Her husband had made a fortune out of gold mines. They had no children, if I remember rightly, and she finished her days being cared for by the Carmelite sisters. As a leading surgeon (urologist), the husband of my wonderful sister, and father of eight remarkable children, Jim remained a huge presence in the life of the whole family. His passing to God on 28 September seemed to be like the going forth of a Viking king from his people. We called him "Big Jim" and he deserved that epithet.

During 2010, I continued to travel: in April to chair a meeting in Oxford for the Templeton Foundation; mid-July to mid-August (right after the World Cup) to lecture in South Africa (in Johannesburg, Bloemfontein, Cape Town and Durban); and then back to the USA in early October (to lecture in San Francisco, New York, and Newport, Rhode Island). During the year I kept up publishing: with Michael Keenan Jones, *Jesus Our Priest* (Oxford University Press) and *Philip Pullman's Jesus* (Darton, Longman & Todd/Paulist Press), as well as producing (with two friends) Tony de Mello's lectures on the *Spiritual Exercises*, published by Doubleday as *Seek God Everywhere*. That work was made more demanding and rewarding by an exigent New York editor who had found Jesus by reading de Mello some years earlier.

I continue to be astonished and deeply grateful at all the kindness I experience on a big scale or a small scale. In mid-September two English friends conspired to give me my first visit to Sydney Opera House—for a dazzling performance of Verdi's *Rigoletto*. When I entered the USA on September 30, the official on passport control decided that, since we were both of Irish origin, there was no need to photograph and fingerprint me and simply waved me on. A month later, back in Melbourne, the governor of Victoria asked me to a dinner with Emperor Hirohito's daughter, now 71 and on a visit with her husband to Melbourne for the BIG race meeting, the Melbourne Cup. She turned out to be very gracious and charming, But she was disappointed, as, unlike two years ago, a Japanese horse failed to win. A French horse, ridden by a French jockey, took the honours.

Christmas 2011

This past year took me away from Melbourne on various occasions: once to Lismore in Northern New South Wales (to lecture to fifty people in education) and once to Perth (to lecture at the University of Western Australia). In August the Templeton Foundation was generous enough to fly me over to Denmark for a meeting of fourteen theologians (on the incarnation) held very close to Hamlet's castle in Elsinore. From our hotel, Marienlyst (which was also the first casino to open in Denmark), we watched a thunder storm break over the castle and saw lightning flashing around the battlements. Statues of Hamlet and Vikings dot the landscape in those parts.

For better or worse, I continue to publish, with the latest major book being *Rethinking Fundamental Theology* (Oxford University Press). In very early 2012 Paulist Press (Mahwah, NJ) will put out my *Believing in the Resurrection*, probably my last book on the subject. [It wasn't. In 2017 Oxford University Press published my *Saint Augustine on the Resurrection of Christ*.] At my late stage of life, I am more concerned now about the practice of resurrection rather than its theory.

For their Christmas number, the London *Tablet* seem to have decided on publishing a piece I wrote on Jesus fiction ("Imagining Jesus"). Since I began writing for the *Tablet* at Easter 1968, it's about time to stop.

Every blessing now to you and all your dear ones at Christmas and in the New Year.

Christmas 2012

Students and colleagues are leaving the Jesuit Theological College for summer assignments and holidays. One is heading south to the Antarctica and will spend a month as a chaplain on a base. He hopes to include a quick visit to the South Pole. Some like it cold! Celebrating a wedding for two friends on December 29 will close the year out for me.

On October 11, the feast of Blessed John XXIII, Catholics and others recalled how fifty years ago he opened the Second Vatican Council. That anniversary has involved me in speaking at conferences (in Sydney and Melbourne) and in two weeks of lecturing in the UK for the diocese of Portsmouth, with one lecture also for Heythrop College (London). I have written articles on Vatican II for various journals: *America*, *The Pastoral Review*, *The Tablet*, and *Theological Studies*. There is more to come! In March 2013, Oxford University Press will publish my *The Second Vatican Council on Other Religions*.

In July, Connor Court of Ballarat (Victoria) (with Gracewing, Leominster) published volume one of my memoirs, *A Midlife Journey*. The former Archbishop of Canterbury, George Carey, wrote a generous foreword. Volume two, covering 1974-2006 and provisionally entitled *On the Left Bank of the Tiber*, will follow soon, to be published by Connor Court (Australia) and Gracewing (UK).

The knights and dames of the Order of Malta keep me busy as a magistral chaplain (celebrating Masses, leading an annual retreat etc.). The Grand Master, Matthew Festing, visited Melbourne briefly and encouraged the members and others (and especially young people) to work for those in need. Some supervision (two long research essays, a master's thesis, and two doctorates) keep my teaching life going. The students are all doing degrees for the MCD University of Divinity.

This year has seen some cherished friends, Cardinal Carlo Maria Martini, Father Peter Steele, and Alec Lynch, go off to God. I wrote obituaries for each of them—in Martini's case, obituaries for three journals.

Christmas 2013

As usual, the year has been punctuated with trips to give lectures: in New South Wales, South Australia, and Western Australia, as well as some trips within Victoria (to Bacchus Marsh and Bendigo). Bacchus Marsh gave me a fascinating entrée into country life in that district, as my brief was to speak at a breakfast for various Christians on the occasion of Father's Day.

On the local scene here in Melbourne, I have continued to celebrate the Eucharist, offer a spiritual retreat, and do other things for the Knights and Dames of Malta. One of them, Richard Divall, in fact the only fully professed Knight of Malta in Australia, has just submitted a doctoral dissertation he wrote on the sacred music of Niccolò Isouard, a Maltese composer born in the late eighteenth century. The dissertation involved producing a professional edition of Isouard's sacred music (something never done before), placing it in the setting of eighteenth-century Malta (still ruled at that time by the Knights of Malta) and evaluating it musically and theologically. John Griffiths, recently retired from a chair in music at the University of Melbourne, proved most generous and valuable as the co-director. I could never have taken on the task of directing Fra' Richard without John's constant help.

Writing and publishing continue. In August, Connor Court put out the Australian edition of the second volume of my memoirs, *On the Left Bank of the Tiber*. At two separate functions in Melbourne, Canon David Richardson (former director of the Anglican Centre in Rome) did the first launch and Tim Fischer (former Australian ambassador to the Holy See) did the second. Whatever you say about the usefulness or otherwise of book launches, they produce good parties with friends and relatives. Both volumes of the memoirs have now appeared in the UK, with Gracewing of Leominster.

One special blessing in 2013 was the chance of lunch with Grace de Mello, the sister of an outstanding Indian spiritual writer, Anthony de Mello, S.J., who died (of a heart attack) too young in 1987. A couple of years ago I retrieved and co-published lectures by Tony on the *Spiritual Exercises* of St Ignatius Loyola. It was happy surprise when I discovered that Grace came to Australia twenty years ago and lives not far away in another suburb of Melbourne.

Christmas 2014

One happy milestone arrived in May when the University of Divinity (Melbourne) awarded Fra' Richard Divall a PhD for his thesis on the sacred music of an 18th century Maltese composer, Niccolò Isouard. After directing to completion over ninety doctoral dissertations at the Gregorian University (Rome), I did not intend to take on again the role of *Doktorvater*, but I am glad to have made two exceptions. [In fact I made three, all for the University of Divinity: Richard, Simon Wayte, and Daryl Barclay.] Richard, an outstanding conductor and editor of music, sacred and profane, has prepared a wonderful CD for the centenary of the Gallipoli campaign in 2015. As the only professed Knight of Malta in Australia, he helps me constantly in my role as one of their three magistral chaplains in Melbourne. That involves frequently celebrating the Eucharist for the sick and elderly, as well as leading the Knights and Dames of Malta on retreats and celebrating the Eucharist with them.

One happy reunion came at an elaborate book launch in the Victorian State Library when Jay Winter presented the three volumes on World War I that he had edited for Cambridge University Press. I first met Jay in the sixties when we were both graduate students at Pembroke College, Cambridge. He has been at Yale for years, and remains the epitome of a wise and gracious historian.

In early May I spoke in the Pumphouse, a Fitzroy pub, to a group of a hundred young people who meet for Theology at the Pub (to be distinguished from Spirituality in the Pub). They asked me to compare and contrast Pope John XXIII and Pope John Paul II, who had both just been canonized in Rome by Pope Francis on April 27.

Lecturing trips have been limited to two cities in Victoria (Ballarat and Bendigo) and to various centres in the Lismore diocese (northern New South Wales). But in early July I did visit New Zealand and spoke to a group of priests, deacons, and seminarians in the Hamilton diocese. A centre, Hobbiton, makes Tolkien's creations seem just around the corner. Through the filming of his books and the arrival of tourists, the locals have enjoyed additional prosperity.

For the year's most zestful human and spiritual experience, my vote has to go to three hundred members of the Calabrian community. In their centre just beyond the main Melbourne airport, I celebrated the Eucharist and led them in a procession (animated by a brass band) in honour of San Rocco. An unusual medieval saint, he cared for the sick up and down the Italian peninsula, caught the plague, but recovered. A large wound in his thigh reminds you of what he suffered. Viva San Rocco! Viva Calabria! Viva l'Italia.

Christmas 2015

This year of grace, 2015, kept me for the most part in Australia. Before Easter I flew north to Singapore and lectured at a theological institute on Christ's resurrection. After Pentecost I flew east to Wellington, New Zealand, and lectured on the Second Vatican Council to the clergy of the Archdiocese. Otherwise, speaking engagements took me to Sydney, Brisbane, and other places in Eastern Australia: above all, three visits for meetings with educationalists and parents in the diocese of Lismore, Northern New South Wales.

Ever since I returned to live in Melbourne in 2009, leaders in education in Lismore have invited me repeatedly to speak to them. As a way of thanking them, I have dedicated to them my latest book, *From Rome to Royal Park* (Connor Court/Gracewing), volume three of my memoirs. It's number 65 of the books I have authored or co-authored since 1965.

The next book, *Revelation: Towards a Christian Theology of God's Self-revelation in Jesus Christ* (Oxford University Press; my twelfth with OUP), should be out before the end of 2016. Some time in 2016, St Paul's in London will publish a biblical/spiritual work, *Letters to Nevie* [a grand-niece].

If I couldn't get to the USA and Europe, friends came from there to stay with me: most recently, Louis Caruana, SJ, the dean of philosophy at the Gregorian University (Rome). Louis included Melbourne in his lecture tour of Australia. A PhD from Cambridge, Louis is a philosopher of science and has insightful things to say about scientific method. During his visit to Oz, his chief base was Australian National University (Canberra). Then Dan Kendall, SJ, a long-standing friend from the University of San Francisco, came and stayed for ten days, en route back to California from lecturing in Macau.

Landmarks punctuated the year: a 90th birthday celebration for my eldest sister Moira; and the 80th birthday dinner for John Batt, a retired judge who has been a friend for sixty years (since we met as students of the classics at the University of Melbourne). Both celebrations were held at the Melbourne Club.

The hospitality and empathy of family and friends provide more than enough support. The present pope makes me think frequently of St

Francis of Assisi, who created the first Christmas crib. He stamped on the world's imagination the place of Christ's birth; an outhouse for animals that is radiant with divine light.

Christmas 2016

This year's 400th anniversary of the death of William Shakespeare naturally brought celebrations and exhibitions around Melbourne. For me, the most informative and enjoyable evening came with the power-point lecture (in English) by a visiting professor from the University of Padua, Alessandra Petrina, currently the president of the Italian Shakespeare Society. Sketching the differences between the University of Bologna (church-dominated) and the University of Padua (student-dominated), she teased out Shakespeare's great interest in Italy, in general, and his references to Padua, in particular. Her visit was sponsored by the Italian Assistance Association (CoAsit, short for Comitato Assistenza Italiana) and the University of Melbourne.

Alas, 2016 did not involve any visits for me to Italy or anywhere else in Europe. In August I did go as far as Auckland (New Zealand) and lectured to the clergy of that diocese on Pope Francis and his exhortation *The Joy of Love*. As Auckland is closer than Perth on the West Australian coast, that visit to New Zealand hardly felt like leaving Oz.

One bit of church news that proved very cheering was Blase Cupich, the Archbishop of Chicago, being created a cardinal by Pope Francis. He studied with me at the Gregorian University, Rome, and later as rector of the Josephinum (Columbus, Ohio) invited me to do a little lecturing in that pontifical university. A few years ago he visited Melbourne on a lecturing tour of Australia and we enjoyed a meal together at Newman College, University of Melbourne.

Sadly this year a dear friend, Richard Divall, has been increasingly invaded by cancer. A legendary conductor of Italian opera, he invited me in September 2015 to the opening night of *Maria Stuarda*. You will remember how at the end the lights go out and there is a terrible thud as Mary loses her head. This year Richard was to conduct another Donizetti opera, *Anna Bolena*, and I was looking forward to a second execution to round off the evening.

Occasional lectures filled up 2016. I also produced two books: *Revelation: Towards a Christian Interpretation of God's Self-Revelation in Jesus Christ* (Oxford University Press) and *Letters to Nevie* (London, St Paul's) to encourage prayerful reading of the Scriptures. Around Easter 2017, Oxford University Press will publish my *Saint Augustine on the Resurrection of Christ*.

Christmas 2017

Years ago the American playwright Tennessee Williams on a visit to Rome spoke proudly of being descended from a brother of St Francis Xavier. While the saint died in the Far East, at least one of his siblings migrated to the Americas and became the ancestor of Williams. "Life is saturated with death" was one of the memorable lines I recall from Williams, and it proved itself true in 2017. In January I preached at the funeral (in St Patrick's Cathedral and with a thousand people present) of Richard Divall and buried him in Melbourne General Cemetery. For twenty years the conductor of opera in Melbourne, Richard became a close friend after I returned to Melbourne in 2009 and began living at the Jesuit Theological College in Parkville only a few hundred metres from his home on Royal Park. In March I did the funeral for my brother Jim, who for years had battled several forms of cancer. In October my sister Moira, the matriarch of our family, died suddenly and we buried her from the chapel of Newman

College, where she had been married in 1946. [As my brother Jim had also been married in that chapel, his funeral took place there.]

But the year was also full of life—not least the chance of christening Alexander and, a week later, Jonathan Charles. For the first time in many years I attended a First Communion, two grandnieces (Susan and Naomi) at their school in Melbourne (called "Genazzano"). Eight tertians (Jesuits in their final year of formation), who came from China, India, Ireland, Japan, the Philippines, and Vietnam, arrived in January and departed in August. Much life also came through leading on a spiritual retreat a group of knights and dames of Malta (March in Pymble, NSW) and a group of priests from the Armidale diocese (November in a motel near Coffs Harbour, also NSW). Right through the year, life came from keeping dementia at bay by writing: in April OUP published my *Saint Augustine on the Resurrection of Christ*, and then, in October, Liturgical Press published a book I did with John Wilkins, *Lost in Translation*. I have just finished dealing with an OUP copy-editor on a work to be published in July 2018, *Inspiration*.

Having written all this about my experience of 2017, I am reminded of T. S. Eliot's "The Journey of the Magi": "Were we led all that way for Birth or Death?" Most years combine both, and 2017 did so in a particular way. A blessed Christmas and grace-filled New Year to you and all your dear ones, Gerald O'Collins.

Christmas, 2018

I am definitely at that time in life when every now and then you indulge big efforts to clean up correspondence and throw out all manner of old scraps. One recent binge unearthed a program for the degree ceremony at the University of Melbourne, March 12, 1958. Among the others receiving a degree (in fact, a MA in education) was Henry Leopold Speagle (what a splendid name!), who already had a MA in the faculty of arts. Long famous as a local specialist in matters liturgical, Henry celebrated his ninetieth birthday this year, and invited a group of friends to a suitable lunch of the "Ancient Anglicans" at the Melbourne Club. That group meets at the Club every first Monday of the month. Their convenor is Alan Gregory, former Master of Ormond College (University of Melbourne) and a very enthusiastic alumnus of Melbourne High School, the school where my Father happily did his final three years of secondary education. Ever since I returned to live in Melbourne in late 2009, the Ancient Anglicans have made me very welcome. Occasionally their archbishop, Philip Freier, who isn't that ancient, turns up. A couple of years back, I invited for lunch with them a visiting Catholic archbishop, George Stack (Cardiff, Wales). The AAs form a genial, relaxed, ecumenical forum.

The knights and dames of Malta continue to supply pastoral engagements: a weekly Eucharist at a day-care centre for Italians and, every now and then, a more elaborate Eucharist (centred on Our Lady of Lourdes) in retirement homes around Melbourne.

Commitment to the cause of teaching the Latin and Greek languages and literature in our high schools and universities involves attending some lectures, including some delivered at formal lunches and dinners. I am down to my last doctoral student [Daryl Barclay], a candidate for the degree from the (ecumenical) University of Divinity, who is the choir director in the Melbourne cathedral, St Patrick's, and a very superior teacher of English literature at a leading high school. I feel myself to be an observer rather than a director of his dissertation (on Jean Pierre de Caussade's sacrament of the moment and also involving Virginia Woolf's Mrs Dalloway).

Last June, friends in the UK sponsored a weekend conference to commemorate the life and work of Michael Hayes, the beloved editor of *The Pastoral Review* who died at Easter 2017. They flew me over to deliver the keynote lecture on Michael. Those few days in England allowed me to catch up with relatives, friends at St Mary's University, and a largish group who attended the summer reception of the London *Tablet* in the courtyard of a church in Chelsea. A blessed Christmas and New Year.

PS Where 2017 sadly saw three deaths (my brother Jim, my sister Moira, and a dear friend and conductor of opera, Richard Divall), 2018 managed to feature the publication of four books: (*Biblical*) *Inspiration* (Oxford University Press), *Tradition* (also OUP), *A Christology of Religions* (Orbis Books), and *Moments of Grace* (Kevin Mayhew).

Christmas 2019

With tongue firmly in his cheek, the Irish genius James Joyce said of John Henry Newman: "nobody has ever written English prose that can be compared with that of a tiresome footling little Anglican parson who afterwards became a prince of the only true Church." It was a great joy to be alive for Newman's canonization on October 13, 2019. I hope and pray for a blazing exception to normal practice, and see Newman's writings prompt his entering the most select group of saints by being officially proclaimed the thirty-seventh Doctor of the Church.

My beloved sister Maev, the only other survivor of my parents' six children, was honoured by Australian Catholic University with an honorary doctorate. I could not share that occasion on 12 April. But I happily visited Canberra to celebrate her ninetieth birthday on 16 June, the famous Bloom's Day of Joyce's *Ulysses*.

As one of their chaplains, the Order of Malta keeps me pastorally engaged with visits to retirement homes around Melbourne and a respite centre for old Italians in Kew. At the end of November, along with Archbishop Jean Laffitte (their official prelate), several of the supreme council of the Order visited from Rome for an Asia Pacific Conference. Laffitte, when a student at the French Seminary, had been my student at the Gregorian University. After not seeing each other for 35 years, he greeted me warmly as "professore."

As the world knows, the annual Melbourne Cup is THE racing event in Australia. This year I attended the Mass—in fact concelebrated—for the racing fellowship in St Francis' Church, Melbourne's oldest, CBD church on November 4, two days before the Cup (always held on the first Tuesday of November). Numerous owners, trainers, jockeys and other concerned folk attended the Mass. Some owners brought along the cups they had won in previous years; inside the sanctuary there was a special table for those cups. The last time I attended the Cup Mass, Michelle Payne (see the film *Ride Like a Girl*) attended in her stylish jockey's outfit and was all set to win the Cup on an outsider (odds of one hundred to one) two days later.

In early 2020 Oxford University Press will publish my *The Beauty of Jesus Christ*. Around the same time, Paulist Press (Mahwah, New Jersey) will put out a book I have co-authored with Daniel Kendall: *Jesuits, Theology, and the American Catholic Church.*

Interest in my maternal grandfather is being promoted by the PM Glynn Institute of Australian Catholic University. This year the institute published Anne Henderson's *Federation's Man of Letters* (Kapunda Press; Connor Court Publishing), which argued that Paddy Glynn's life, inspiration, intellectual heroes, and ideas remain powerfully relevant in debates that continue about Australia's identity and future. One of the founding fathers of Australian federation, until 1919 he remained in the national parliament and was a cabinet minister in several governments. In September, on the occasion of a visit to Australia, Rowan Williams delivered in Sydney the annual PM Glynn lecture.

A blessed Christmas and every grace in the New Year, Gerald O'C.

Part VII:
Pre-pandemic and Pandemic Letters
(2017–2020)

[All of these letters, like the Christmas letters in Part VI, were written from Jesuit Theological College, Parkville, Victoria 3052, Australia.]

August 3, 2017.

[To my sister Maev]

Dearest Maev, Last Tuesday a visiting Italian professor (now with a chair at Villanova University, near Philadelphia) came for the evening meal; he has the splendid name of Massimo Faggioli, which you might translate as Biggest Beans. He is an exuberant person, and has been out lecturing in Sydney, Melbourne, and Adelaide. His favourite topics are Pope Francis and the Second Vatican Council, and he has me writing a chapter for a large book he is editing, *The Oxford Handbook of Vatican II.*

It's certainly the season for visitors from the Northern Hemisphere, with Steve, Marianne, and Samantha through for a long weekend en route to skiing in New Zealand. Last Friday Steve spoke during the students' dinner at Newman College (marking the start of the second semester) on being an engineer in Cambodia. His speech also included items concerned with the setting up of a national rugby team in Cambodia.

For years I have collected ads featuring the theme of "life." The latest one turned up recently at the Melbourne airport. It featured a medical doctor saying: "I'm not just a GP. I'm your life specialist." I continue to read the poems of Clive James, who has been dying on stage now for several years. He's a man who has nothing but poetry left.

I have just corrected the proofs for two books, with one more set of proofs to come imminently. They will lift my score of books published to 71, which is clearly excessive, if not obsessive.

Much love, Gerald.

June 9, 2019.

[To my grandniece, for whom *Letters to Nevie* (see Christmas letters of 2015 and 2016) was written.]

Dear Nevie, Yes, I intend to see *All is True* at the Cinema Nova. The Bard was much loved by Patrick McMahon Glynn, your great-great-grandfather and one of the founding fathers of the Australian Commonwealth. Next Thursday the PM Glynn Institute (of the Australian Catholic University, Sydney) launches at the Athenaeum Club (Collins Street, Melbourne) a book in collaboration about him, *Federation's Man of Letters, Patrick McMahon Glynn*. The main speaker, who also contributed the long, biographical essay at the heart of the book, will be Anne Henderson. She is a political biographer, who has published lives of Enid Lyons [first woman elected to the Australian House of Representatives and the first woman to serve in the federal cabinet], Joseph Lyons [husband of Enid, and Australian Prime Minister 1932–39], and others. You might have read Anne's husband, Gerard Henderson, who writes every now and then for *The Australian*. Jim and Sally [Nevie's parents] are coming to the launch, at which I will speak, albeit briefly.

The other day I wrote to Sally Capp, the Lord Mayor of Melbourne, thanking her for what she does and making a request for Lygon Street, the Italian golden mile just across the campus of Melbourne University from me. Last December, instead of the banners along the street that wished you "Buon natale," some neutral decorations (Christmas crackers) went up. I asked the Lord Mayor to give us back at Christmas the Italian banners, which I hope have not been destroyed. Viva Italia! Viva Lygon Street.

You ask about differences between Sydney and Melbourne. Did you know that in the CBD of Melbourne we have thirty bee hives and in central Melbourne 130 hives? I can't imagine that happening in Sydney, although I am not sure. I can't be sure either about the taste of the honey from Melbourne's city hives.

The Queen Victoria Market is to have a make-over costing one hundred million dollars. Well and good, but I hope this up-grading is not going to destroy the charm that draws me there on many Saturdays to buy pasta. The authorities are keeping in mind how the Queen Vic is a tourist attraction, a factor that should preserve its splendid, heritage features.

Here at the Jesuit Theological College, two seminarians—we call them scholastics—will be ordained priests next Saturday, with the ceremony taking place in St Ignatius Church, Richmond. Alas, I will be away in Canberra, celebrating the 90th birthday of Maev [my sister]. Much love, Gerald.

March 15, 2020.

[To the London *Tablet* but not published.]

After graduating as a paramedic in 2019 at the Australian Catholic University (Melbourne), William ("Billy") Peters, a grand-nephew of mine, accepted a job with the London paramedics. He began work at the end of January, just in time for the arrival of the corona virus. These uniquely busy and sometimes tragic months have pushed Billy to the limit of his resources. But he has been mightily encouraged by the British public repeatedly demonstrating their gratitude to all health-care workers. Last week this support was dramatically confirmed for him in a very personal way. He lost his wallet in a London pub.

The lady who picked it up found inside his American Express Card and his utterly essential driver's licence, but no contact details for Billy. The wallet contained, however, the card of his father, a Melbourne barrister James Peters, QC. Her e-mail to Billy's dad produced instant results. Billy went at once, with enormous relief and gratitude, to retrieve his precious wallet from a London stranger—now more dedicated than ever to his work in London as a paramedic. PS Yes, Billy has been infected by the virus, but, being in his early twenties, shook it off easily.

March 29, 2020.

[To my nephew Frank O'Collins, Sydney.]

Dear Frank, We don't have a lockdown in Melbourne, but often people are short on the streets, with only a few scuttling about. Right here on Royal Parade in Parkville, the shutting of a redbrick church for members of a community of St Thomas Christians has made our Sunday mornings much quieter and less colourful. A few years ago they bought a church that had been built around 1900 on the model of an old church in Scotland and served as a place of worship for local Presbyterians, members of Ormond College (just across Royal Parade), and latterly a few members of the Uniting Church of Australia. At the Jesuit community, 157—175 Royal Parade, we found our Sunday brightened by cars arriving from around Melbourne, flocks of Indian ladies in saris (with the men often dressed much more casually), and bunches of small children. They began at 9 am or earlier and continued all Sunday morning, using the church itself and the adjacent lawn. Twenty or so teenagers would come to one of our terrace buildings, 175 Royal Parade, and occupy a classroom for their lessons in catechism. Recently the Indians invited our rector to preach at a Sunday morning liturgy. All in all, those St Thomas Christians made our Sundays lively, festive occasions. Now Sunday morning seems thoroughly sombre.

I have been collecting poems and prayers that the corona virus has prompted. You must have read "Lockdown" by Richard Hendrick, OFM, which turned up on the BBC recently and has followed the virus around the world: "Yes, there is fear. Yes there is isolation. Yes there is panic buying. Yes there is sickness. Yes there is even death. But. They say that in Wuhan after so many years of noise/You can hear the birds again. They say that after a few weeks of quiet/The sky is no longer thick with fumes/But blue and grey and clear. They say that in the streets of Assisi/People are singing to each other/ across the empty squares..."

The latest prayers often don't quite live up that standard. In the present, viral situation, I still like best a prayer from St Anselm of Canterbury (d. 1109): "God of love, whose compassion never fails, we bring before you the troubles and perils of people and nations, the sighing of prisoners and captives, the sorrows of the bereaved, the necessities of strangers, the helplessness of the weak, the despondency of the weary, the failing powers of the aged. O Lord, draw near to each; for the sake of Jesus Christ our Lord."

Some of my friends have turned back to reading again Albert Camus's *The Plague*. What I recall most and recall sadly about the novel is that, after all the fears and deaths abate, the survivors hardly seem to have been changed by their experiences of a city in lockdown for months. Peace and love, Gerald.

March 30, 2020.

[To Gesine and Massimiliano Doria Pamphilj, Rome.]

Dear Gesine, Massimiliano and all your dear ones, Hearing the news from Italy and the terrible toll the corona virus has already taken, I have been thinking of you and praying for you. Here in Melbourne we are blessed with three interesting heavenly patrons or at least temporary patrons: St Thérèse of Lisieux and her two (canonized) parents. Some time back their relics left France on a world tour, and reached Melbourne just as the corona virus began causing lockdowns. Now the relics remain for an undetermined time in the local Carmelite monastery. May the saintly Martin family roll back the virus and its impact from this city!

You must have seen Pope Francis in St Peter's Square last Friday. It looked so strange, even surreal, to watch him walking alone through the wet and deserted square—a tiny, white figure in the darkness. He excelled himself with the homily and its message, "with God life never dies."

I hope and pray, Gesine, that the cancer has diminished or even disappeared. You might remember in your prayers my sister Maev, now ninety and living hundreds of miles away in Canberra. She has generous and loving neighbours, but I wish she was down here in Melbourne where most of her close relatives live. I spend my time doing some translation work—specifically, putting into English some passages from documents from the Second Vatican Council— and writing articles. It's all a good distraction from the general nervousness that the corona virus has caused, Much love to each of you, Gerald.

April 21, 2020.

[To Josef and Ingrid Nolte, Tübingen, Germany.]

Dear Josef, Ingrid, and all your dear ones, I hope all goes well, despite the corona virus. I think we're stuck with this virus for a long haul, but it only makes friends like you even more precious. In January a grandnephew, Billy Peters, arrived in London to begin work as paramedic; he graduated a year ago from the Australian Catholic University and the authorities in the UK are happy with the courses at ACU. He is coping with an extraordinary start to his career— much encouraged by the ways the British public is expressing thanks to health care workers. A nephew (Steve), an engineer in his early fifties who has worked for years on waste management in South-East Asia and lives (with wife and daughter) in Malaysia, is flat out designing ways of disposing safely (and maybe profitably) of COVID-19 waste for the Asian Development Bank.

While Billy and Steve are at the front, I am locked away in the Jesuit Theological College with seven others, including one who graduated in medicine before becoming a Jesuit. It is reassuring to live next door to a doctor at this viral time. Two of the other Jesuits were lawyers before they entered the Society, and have been keeping the rest of us accurate and informed in what we discuss about the Cardinal George Pell case. He was hardly acquitted 7/0 by the Australian High Court, before someone else apparently (police leak!) contacted the police about another offence allegedly committed in the 1970s. No doubt about our coppers; they will not quit on getting their man.

A youngish American friend, a lay theologian, sent me, for Easter, links to recordings of nine heavy metal, Christian bands. A kind gesture, but I cannot remember ever showing interest in heavy metal bands, Christian or otherwise.

I potter away writing articles of a biblical nature for the *Expository Times* and other journals. It's a case of "il primo amore non si scorda mai (one's first love never becomes unravelled)". I prefer the Italian to the English version of this saying; it brings out love's activity, rather than its memory ("you never forget your first love"). Scriptures were my first love, and so I've come back to them.

Oxford University Press publish this month my *The Beauty of Jesus Christ*. With warmest Easter greetings, affection and prayer, Gerald.

May 17, 2020.

[To Mary Venturini, living now on Jersey.]

Dear Mary,

A very grace-filled feast of the Ascension next Thursday. Years ago you wrote such a wonderful section on the Ascension for *Believing* [a book we published together in 1991]; I sensed that it was a special liturgical feast for you.

You must know the Beaulieu Convent School? I think an old friend of mine, Paul Rowan, is still there. We met in Rome and then caught up at St Mary's University College, Strawberry Hill.

Despite the pandemic, Dr Willie Campbell (yes, he was born in Scotland where he also did his basic training in medicine), who lasered my left eye three months ago, has not shut up shop. Last week he lasered my right eye, and now both eyes enable me to read happily and without glasses. Am I grateful for the progress of medicine and the skill of Willie, who served as a resident under my late brother Jim (the head surgeon of a Melbourne hospital) after migrating years ago to Australia!

At this Jesuit precinct opposite the University of Melbourne, we continue to see the best of films and engage in thoughtful discussions that may train us to be top (or maybe only mediocre) cinema critics. On Friday evening it was "The King", a kind of alternative to Shakespeare's "Henry V." Impossible to see without thinking of the classical performances of Kenneth Branagh and Laurence Olivier as H. V., the film did its job under an Australian director and was shot in Hungary.

During the reign of the virus, I am able to catch up with a favourite BBC Sunday program, "Songs of Praise". Last Sunday a Coptic church in London was on; the Sunday before the program took us to Tenby beach and the very old (fifth century) monastery on Caldey Island, off the coast of Wales.

Peace, love and Ascension blessings to you, Gerry.

June 14, 2020.

[To Monsignor Bernard McGarty, La Crosse, Wisconsin.]

Dear Bernie, Many thanks for your card, which gives me this chance of contacting you. First of all, my deep condolences and prayers on the death of your dear and wonderful sister. R.I.P. I remain immensely grateful to you for bringing me to Wisconsin. Those visits from the early nineties up to 2006 were full of grace and joy for me.

These days of lock-down in the face of the pandemic are not what I expected from 2020. But there have been the lovely items, like a priest from Shanghai who joined my birthday celebration and sang in mandarin "happy birthday to you". The tune, by the way, is the same. The government, if slowly, is lifting restrictions. The Melbourne Zoo, just north of where I live, is re-opened; the animals must have missed us and demanded our return. But, since the number of visitors is limited and you go on line to book a ticket, signs en route to the zoo warn those who have not yet booked with the message "ZOO FULL."

Oxford University Press has just published my *The Beauty of Jesus Christ*. So I have started on another book for them—eighteen articles on New Testament topics which I authored or co-authored over the years. For the first five years after completing my PhD, I taught the letters of St Paul, along with a course in fundamental theology, for Weston School of Theology (then Cambridge, Massachusetts). But departmental arrangements meant that I had to stay with the theologians (fundamental and systematic) when I moved to Rome; nevertheless, every now and then I published a scriptural article in *Biblica, Catholic Biblical Quarterly, Expository Times* or some other journal. So I am revising the earlier pieces and bringing them up to date. More than half appeared in recent years and hardly call for any retouching. Provisionally, I am calling this collection: *Expounding the New Testament: The Gospels, Acts and Paul.* As Oxford University Press declined to take the book, I am negotiating with another publishing house.

Thanks again for everything, and all the very, very best in the good Lord.

PS Paulist Press will shortly publish a book I co-authored: *Jesuits, Theology and the American Catholic Church*. You will know some of those recalled in it.

July 28, 2020.

[To Lady Primrose Potter, Melbourne.]

Dear Primrose,

Well, here we are five months down the pandemic track in defending ourselves against the "opportunistic psychopath" as one journalist has described the corona virus. Dan Andrews [the premier of the State of Victoria] went for alliteration when he denounced Covid-19 as a "very complex, cunning, and clever enemy." But should one personify a virus? Whatever we say, I hope you are well and truly guarded against the enemy.

Advice, prayers and quotations have arrived in a steady stream through my computer. A quote received recently comes from A. A. Milne, *Winnie the Pooh*: "Promise me you will always remember you're braver than you believe, and stronger than you seem, and smarter than you think." Covid-time has proved cliché-time. Yet some sentiments appeal: "the role of economic forecasting is to make astrology seem respectable."

The pandemic makes some ads unconsciously amusing, like one (in *The Economist*) for a property in Tuscany: "don't just own it. Live it. Now is your chance to create a life in the real Tuscany, in a land untouched by time." In 2021 we will celebrate 700 years since the death of Dante. I wonder what he would think about Tuscany being a land untouched by time. It's precisely because it is a land touched by time that it's so interesting and beautiful.

Furthermore, what on earth is the unreal Tuscany, as opposed to the real Tuscany?

Yesterday in an e-mail my nephew Jim Peters quoted to me something very apposite from Catullus. I started noting his preference for the Latin lyric poets when he first visited me in Rome and wanted to see the places that inspired Horace. I am firmly in the epic camp of Virgil: "sunt lacrimae rerum et mentem mortalia tangunt." It sounds banal in English: "there are tears for things (human affairs??) and mortal things touch the mind" ("heart" might be better).

Covid-time is making me more alert to quirky bits of information like a Brisbane church built of concrete in the 1960s, which has just won "the Enduring Architecture Award" in the annual assignment of Queensland architecture awards. That seems a tautology, or is an oxymoron involved? If the building is made of concrete, it should be sturdily there fifty or sixty years down the track.

Peace, love and good cheer, Gerald.

August 2020 (a round robin).

Life in plague-town has done wonders for my writing. I have been inspired by the example of the Russian Pushkin (holed up in the countryside during a cholera epidemic and coming up with Eugene Onegin) and the Italian Boccaccio, faced with the black death but producing his best work. Maybe it's not my best but I have put together 18 articles (that I have published over nearly fifty years) on the Gospels, the Acts of the Apostles and themes of St Paul. The concluding chapter tells the story of how an article published in 1971 (on Paul's notion of divine power made perfect in his human weakness (2 Corinthians 12:9-10)) was subsequently received, rejected or modified by biblical scholars. One of these was a German who treated me better than I deserved, probably since I engaged with an overwhelmingly German squad in my article. This latest opus from me is now being assessed by an American publisher.

Life in lock-downed Melbourne has also started me reading some of the personal letters of St Ignatius Loyola and continuing my reading of Julian Barnes. Why didn't I pick up those letters years ago? They provide exceptionally vivid insights into the life and thinking of the founder of the Jesuits. As the pandemic broke, I was well into Barnes' latest, a tour de force built around the life of surgeon, Samuel Pozzi, whose portrait by John Singer Sargent provides the title: *The Man in the Red Coat*. Among Pozzi's merits—but there were also some serious demerits—was his defence of Dreyfus, the victim of a gross personal injustice.

As a reviewer has noted, the Dreyfusard Paris of 1909 sounds uncannily like Melbourne in 2019. This book prompted me into seeing again the film based on Barnes' *A Sense of an Ending*, which might be summed up by a line from his older friend (only acquaintance?), Philip Larkin: "what will remain of us is love" (quote accurate?). Next I plunged into Barnes' account of the inner struggles of Shostakovich, *The Noise of Time*. I have long wondered why the Russian composer resisted until Stalin's death the pressure to join the Communist party, but then did so when a thaw came under Khrushchev. Barnes supplies a satisfying explanation. Incidentally, you are more than halfway through the book before you learn the reason for the title: "art is the whisper of history, heard above the noise of time" (p. 91 in my paperback edition). Barnes returns to this language a little later: "the music of our being ... if it is strong and pure enough to drown out the noise of time, is transformed into the whisper of history" (p. 125).

Our state premier is continuing his practice of personifying

Covid-19, saying that 'it is a silent enemy and a very cunning enemy."
What would Virgil think of this practice? That's a question for Jim
Peters [a barrister nephew] and myself as we continue to swop
quotations from the Aeneid.

[To Jürgen Moltmann, Tübingen.]

August 17, 2020.

Dear Jürgen,

I hope all has gone well for you, and all your dear ones. As you will
have seen in the news, Melbourne is back to a more severe lockdown,
involving a curfew (8 pm to 5 am), wearing masks, and soldiers on
the streets to enforce these and other regulations. Through the
window of my second-floor study, I have just seen an army patrol
pass by.

Last week I was one of the ten persons allowed to attend the requiem
Mass of a New Zealand friend, celebrated in a large suburban church.
Everyone was masked, including Michael Tobin, the well preserved,
silky white-haired, now semi-retired director of an agency who for
many years has presided over the funerals of numerous relatives and
friends of mine.

Always in a perfect suit, with a matching tie and handkerchief,
Michael fits his role perfectly.

But last week even he could not manage to look the part. The mask
distracted you totally from his formal "uniform".

With all outside activities, including visits to relatives and friends,
forbidden, I have been driven to do more reading and writing.
Fortunately, some invitations from editors have come along to

satisfy the urge to write. The latest request asked for 6,000 words on what my theology has achieved. Answering such a request looks daunting in the extreme. But at least I can confirm that teaching and writing theology have kept me contented. Declaring what that activity has done for others lurches into the controversial.

A desire to read has taken me back to Homer and Virgil. I started with the *Iliad* but then switched to the *Aeneid*. You remember its opening words, "arma virumque cano (I sing of arms and the man"), which years ago were adopted as the motto of the classics department at the University of Melbourne and appeared on their stationery? Some truly ignorant individual in search of a teaching position took the words to be the full name of the professor who headed the department and opened his letter by writing: "Dear Professor Cano". Needless to say, he was not taken on.

An abundance of time has also prompted me into reading novels I have kept in my room but never opened. As of now I have finished the first of a quartet by Martin Boyd, an Australian writer who eventually lived near the Trevi Fountain and died in Rome in 1979. Daffodils, mimosa and other flowers, as well as sunny days, are signalling that spring is on the way. The sooner the summer arrives to check the corona virus, the better.

In alter Freundschaft, Gerry.

September 23, 2020.

[To Revd Michael Keenan Jones, PP, Shelton, CT, co-author with me of *Jesus Our Priest*.]

Dear Mike, I hope you and all your dear family have been doing ok in these best of times and worst of times.

Prompted by a friend, a former speech writer for Malcolm Fraser, I have been trying to come up with a popular song to lift the spirits of people who are suffering from lockdown blues. So far only a few words have popped into my head to match a tune taken from "Men of Harlech": "Team Australia, do your share, keep the rules and show you care, not for profit or for gain but for Oz's name. Aussies, Aussies, Aussies, Aussies, show that you are tried and true ones..."

I have been doing better collecting inspirational lines: "Some old-fashioned things like fresh air and sunshine are hard to beat." "We do not know what the future holds, but we do know who holds the future."

Here in the Parkville precinct, with eight other Jesuits (two lawyers, two other Anglos, one Chinese, and three Vietnamese, one of whom is a medical doctor), I have seen over six months of restricted living in our plague city slip by. One Anglo member of the community who normally spends part of a weekend in a very busy parish in the Western suburbs of Melbourne confessed that he has been feeling imprisoned. That prompted a big smile from one of the Vietnamese. After the fall of Saigon, having belonged to the elite South Vietnamese marine corps, he spent three years in a concentration camp before escaping on a boat. "In the camp," he recalled, "they shouted at you, went in for torture, and kept you at forced labour. The food was terrible and, if you played soccer against the guards, you had to make sure you lost. That's what it can mean to be imprisoned."

Outside my kitchen, the red-flowering camellia has been a blaze of blooms, the best I have seen it in ten years. Since camellias were called after a Jesuit botanist (Georg Joseph Kamel) and flourish in Vietnam and China, our specimen may be registering its approval of the presence of the Vietnamese and Chinese Jesuits here on Royal Parade.

The other day I wrote (but have not sent) a letter to Rupert Murdoch, asking for support for an ecumenical, educational project here in Melbourne. My problem is getting the letter into his hands; if I am to receive a NO, at least let it come from the man himself and not from someone else well down the line. My deceased brother Jim, by the way, looked after Rupert's mother medically. Any suggestions about how I might get my letter to him would be very welcome.

All the very best in the good Lord, Gerry.

September 27, 2020.

[To Billy Peters and his partner, London. I mention his aunt, Marion Peters.]

Dear Billy and Emma, I hope all is going at least tolerably well in London town. Down here in Melbourne I ply myself with sayings from Pope Francis (e.g. "faith is not a light which scatters all our darkness but a lamp which guides our steps") and the motto of Xavier Jesuit School Cambodia ("Dare to dream of a brighter future"). I find that motto courageous and moving, especially after hearing from Jesuit friends who work in South-East Asia. They persistently picture Cambodia as currently the most difficult and dangerous mission in that part of the whole world.

During the mini-break that came just before the current extreme lockdown, a young couple were married in our chapel here at the Jesuit Theological College. They turned up the other day with their lasting thanks in the form of a largish bush. With the help of Ai, one of our Vietnamese, I planted it in the front garden, right outside 159 Royal Parade and facing the steady flow of students to and from Melbourne University and nurses (to and from the Royal Melbourne Hospital) who continue to make their masked way up and down Royal Parade.

Yesterday the department of theology and religious studies at the University of San Francisco held a memorial service for Dan Kendall, who was on the faculty there since 1979.

Marion stood in for me, and read what I wanted to say about Dan, my first doctoral student in Rome and one with whom I did a lot of publishing over the years. As they have lived for years in San Francisco. Marion and Rick were able to see a lot of Dan.

Last Sunday evening I switched on the opening instalment of the next series of 'Grantchester'—an act of pure nostalgia, since, while the young vicar is stationed a few miles out of Cambridge, most of the action took place at the University and, specifically, at Newnham College (with both the victim and the killer being students there). Among the alumnae of Newnham, Emma Thomson, Germaine Greer and our cousin Jane Ellison would all have been tempted to extreme language if they happened to have seen this instalment. It's not that several students from St John's College came out better. But there was no need to rubbish Newnham in that way.

I can't wait to catch up with you again. Much love, Gerald.

Relatives Mentioned in the Letters

My parents, Patrick Francis O'Collins (d. 1961) and Joan O'Collins (née Glynn; d. 1977).

My eldest sister, Moira Peters (d. 2017), her husband James ("Jim," d. 2010), their children: Stewart (married to Nola), Marion (married to Eric "Rick") Brown; their daughter Abigail, Justin (married to Jill), Joanna (married to Bob Hirth; their children Douglas and Adelaide), Mark, Bronwen (married to Andrew Gould), James ("Jim," married to Sally Ninham); their children, Marion, Genevieve ("Nevie"), Susan and Naomi), and Stephen ("Steve," married to Marianne Lim); and their daughter Samantha.

My second sister, Dympna (d. 2004), her husband Kevin Coleman (d. 1975), their children: Les, Nicholas, Dympna Mary, and Dominic (d. 2019).

My third sister, Maev.

My younger brother Jim (d. 2017), his wife Rosemary ("Posey"); their children: James ("Jamie") and Victoria ("Tori").

My youngest brother, Glynn (d. 2003), his first wife Stephanie (d. 1988), his second wife Barbara; his children by Stephanie: Francis ("Frank"), Stephanie, Ellie, Phillippa, William ("Will").

Index